GARDENWALKS

IN NEW ENGLAND

Help Us Keep This Guide Up to Date

Every effort has been made by the authors and editors to make this guide as accurate and useful as possible. However, many things can change after a guide is published—establishments close, phone numbers change, facilities come under new management, etc.

We would love to hear from you concerning your experiences with this guide and how you feel it could be improved and kept up to date. While we may not be able to respond to all comments and suggestions, we'll take them to heart and we'll also make certain to share them with the authors. Please send your comments and suggestions to the following address:

The Globe Pequot Press
Reader Response/Editorial Department
P.O. Box 480
Guilford, CT 06437

Or you may e-mail us at: editorial@GlobePequot.com

Thanks for your input, and happy travels!

GARDENWALKS SERIES

GARDENWALKS

IN NEW ENGLAND

Beautiful Gardens from Maine to Connecticut

MARINA HARRISON *and* LUCY D. ROSENFELD

INSIDERS' GUIDE®

GUILFORD, CONNECTICUT
AN IMPRINT OF THE GLOBE PEQUOT PRESS

Garden admission fees and hours are subject to change. We recommend that you contact establishments before traveling to obtain current information.

INSIDERS' GUIDE®

Copyright © 2005 by Marina Harrison and Lucy Rosenfeld

Text design by Diane Gleba Hall
Illustrations and maps by Ted Enik

Library of Congress Cataloging-in-Publication Data

Harrison, Marina, 1939–
    Gardenwalks in New England/Marina Harrison and Lucy D. Rosenfeld—1st ed.
        p. cm.—(Gardenwalks series) (Insiders' guide)
    Includes index.
    ISBN 0-7627-3664-X
        1. Gardens—New England—Guidebooks. 2. New England—Guidebooks.
    I. Rosenfeld, Lucy D., 1939– II. Title. III. Series. IV. Series: Insiders' guide

    SB466.U6N426 2005
    712'.0974—dc22

                                                    2004060725

Manufactured in the United States of America
First Edition/First Printing

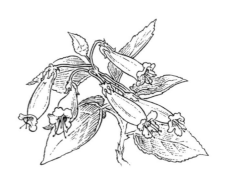

Contents

Preface

*T*HIS BOOK invites garden lovers to join us in a search for beautiful and interesting sights. While we don't pretend to be horticulturalists, botanists, or even to have very green thumbs ourselves, we do know an aesthetic treat when we see one!

As you may know from our previous guidebooks, we are inveterate walkers and connoisseurs of exceptional art and scenery. The 101 gardens we have selected in the New England region provide both natural and aesthetic pleasures. We describe in some detail our favorite gardens, which reflect the melting-pot aspects of our nation, ranging in style from the most eccentric personal expressions to the traditional formal elegance of European and Asian origins. We have not overlooked natural and wildflower preserves, which some people consider the best gardens of all. Also included are sculpture and architectural gardens; conservatories and indoor gardens; specialty gardens, such as an all-peony garden; gardens for the disabled; Asian gardens; gardens with great views, whose very settings make them special; and some intriguing private gardens, whose owners have graciously invited visitors. You'll find at the end of each state chapter a heading called "Don't Miss . . .", which features write-ups of other worthy garden sites.

We have tried to introduce our readers to various historic, multinational, and artistic garden designs in a chapter at the beginning of the book called "Thoughts on Garden Styles." Near the end of the book is "Choosing an Outing," a guide that will help you select a garden to visit by style or tradition.

Every garden in this book is open to the public on a more or less regular basis in season; we have not included gardens open only one day a year. While we cannot—in a useful, portable guide—fully describe every choice garden, we have given a thumbnail sketch of those you should not miss as you travel around New England.

We have spent several years visiting every sort of garden in every season—on beautiful sunny days as well as in pouring rain. Wherever we have gone, we have been given enthusiastic and helpful suggestions. Many people have directed us to gardens we might have overlooked, and others have recommended books and garden tours and have even led us to hard-to-find places themselves.

Gardens are by definition fragile. As living environments they are subject to the whims and changes of nature—and nurture. As we wrote this book, all the gardens we describe were in good condition and welcomed visitors. We hope you will find them as pleasing and carefully tended as we have.

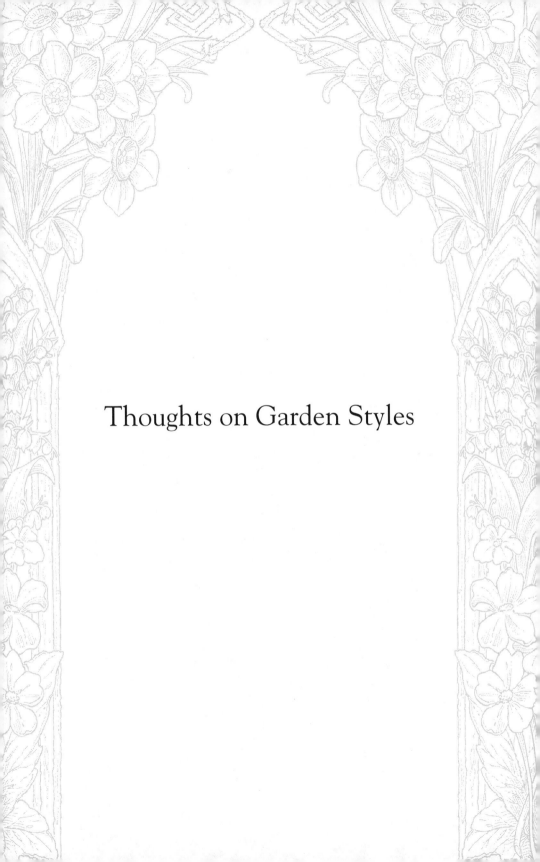

Thoughts on Garden Styles

Formal and Informal Gardens

> "Romanticism" is an idea which needed a Classical mind
> to have it.
>
> —J. F. SHADE (1898–1959)

AMONG THE fundamental questions that have defined land-scape design in America and other Western countries is the issue of formal versus naturalistic gardens. Should a garden focus on structure and architecture or on its plantings? Should it be arranged in geometric patterns, or in a flowing, more random manner reflecting a natural landscape?

The formal approach has its cultural roots in the traditions of Italy and France. Formal gardens in the Italian and French style share important similarities. Both are regarded as architectural extensions of the house; both emphasize structure, symmetry, and classical motifs, such as statues and balustraded terraces; and in both, plants are considered subordinate to the overall design.

The first Italian gardens (as we know them today) appeared during the Renaissance, especially in the regions surrounding Florence and Rome, where some of the most important patrons, sculptors, and architects lived and worked. Villas were built as rural retreats from the city, much like their predecessors in antiquity. Their gardens, linking the house to the surrounding countryside, were designed to be ideal sites for contemplating and experiencing nature. At carefully chosen sites, viewers were invited to enjoy sweeping vistas of the formal layout and the countryside beyond.

The ideal Italian Renaissance garden—elegant, proportioned, and symmetrical—represented a harmonious balance between nature and architecture. Here nature was tamed and ordered into neatly clipped evergreens of laurel, box, and yew shaped into elaborate mazes and borders. Stone and marble forms—colonnaded stairways, terraces, and statues depicting allegorical and mythological characters—were essential elements of this style. So too was water. The Villa d'Este at Tivoli, with its spectacular fountains, cascades, and basins—and amazing waterpowered mechanisms—is one of the most magnificent Renaissance gardens of all.

The Medici family of Florence helped introduce Italian garden designs to France, as did migrating Italian artisans and gardeners. The formal gardens of seventeenth-century France represented a new interpretation of these ideals. To a substantially greater degree than Italian gardens, these totally controlled landscapes symbolized humanity's mastery of the natural world.

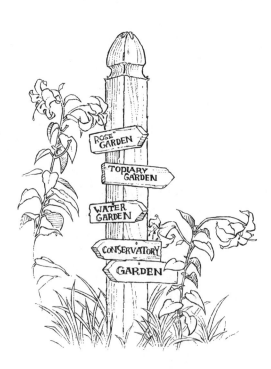

Essential to French formal gardens were ornamental garden beds (parterres) fashioned from exquisitely shaped boxwood and yew. These intricate geometric compartments with squares, circles, and ovals were flawless in their symmetrical designs. They could be viewed from the formal reception rooms of the house overlooking them, or along an orderly grid of walkways. Sometimes complementing them were rows of small trees or shrubs shaped into topiary forms. (Topiaries in Italy tended to represent whimsical creatures, while those in France were strictly geometric and abstract.)

Versailles, the great masterpiece of André Le Nôtre, is certainly the most noted garden in the French style. Everything in it was laid out to symbolize the triumph of humanity (more specifically, the Sun King) over nature, from its majestic proportions and perspectives, to the central axis leading to broad vistas, to the grand canals, fountains, and heroic statues.

In contrast to the formality and symmetry of the continental garden, the English arcadian landscape was a dramatic return to nature. Influenced by romantic landscape painting and the glory of ancient ruins, English garden designers in the eighteenth century sought to re-create a sense of nature's free, wild beauty. Instead of the classical elegance of geometric perspective, orderly planting beds, walkways, and rectangular reflecting pools, the English garden turned to poetic disorder, to free-form designs, even to reconstructed ruins and grottoes—in short, to the garden as a metaphor for romantic poetry and art. Its aim was the "picturesque."

"All gardening is landscape painting," remarked the first great English landscape designer, William Kent. It was Capability Brown and Humphry Repton, however, who created the arcadian landscapes of the great English country houses. In their designs the garden became landscape, a rolling vista that combined hills and fields, clumps of trees, rushing water, poetic lakes, and everywhere distant views. The flower garden was replaced by the beauties of landscape. There are "three aspects of landscape gardening," wrote William Shenstone, "the sublime, the beautiful, and the melancholy or pensive."

The "English garden" as we know it evolved from these poetic landscapes. The flower garden near the house made a comeback in the nineteenth century, replacing the vast green lawns just beyond the door. With a new emphasis on color and an abundance of what appeared to be (though not at all) disordered plantings in mixed species, the glorious flower beds that we think of as English became popular. This style of informal "cottage garden" swept into fashion and could be seen everywhere—from the terraces of grand houses of Britain to Monet's gardens at Giverny. The return of flower gardens and the Victorian interest in the exotic and the extravagant led to increasing use of imported plants, rare flowers, and "the gardenesque"—a deliberately near-chaotic approach to landscape.

To Americans, gifted with spectacular landscapes of a "natural paradise," most thoughts of French formality seemed irrelevant. As Americans first moved beyond their careful, colonial-style gardens into the realm of larger pleasure gardens, many were surely influenced by the English style. Americans with large estates, as well as those planning the first public parks, tried to incorporate natural landscape wonders into their own garden designs. Picturesque gardens were nestled into areas like the magnificent Palisades along the Hudson River, their dramatic settings adding to both design and ambience.

As the great era of wealth in the late nineteenth century brought increased travel abroad, America's new rich familiarized themselves with the elegant French and Italian landscape. Castles rivaling those of Europe were constructed in places like Newport and Philadelphia. Surrounding them were great formal gardens, patterned after Versailles or other grand continental wonders. To the owners of the American palaces, the French garden seemed the epitome of grandeur, the free-form English garden a less elegant option.

As you visit gardens today, you'll find distinct examples of both continental formality and the English "picturesque." But in many cases, particularly in gardens designed in the more recent past, you'll see a mixture of styles and influences that is typical of so many of our contemporary arts. Borrowing liberally from the varied ideas of the past, today's gardens might include formality and fountains as well as free-form planting beds and abstract contemporary sculpture. Exotic plantings, so prized by Victorians, might grow alongside a traditional Roman wall, or a geometric reflecting pool might be edged with contemporary tile. The postmodern emphasis on using elements from diverse sources has not escaped the world of landscape design. Thus, the debate between English informality and continental formality has all but passed into garden history, like the artificial grotto, the ha-ha, and the topiary maze.

The Colonial Garden

> Let every house be placed if the Person pleases in the
> middle of its plot so that there may be found on each side
> for Gardens or Orchards, or fields, so that it may be a
> green Country Town . . . and will always be wholesome.
> —WILLIAM PENN

COLONIAL GARDENS are an important part of America's cultural heritage, and one of its most delightful. Scattered about the East Coast, from New England to the South, they represent a particular time in our history. Whether authentic seventeenth- and eighteenth-century gardens, replicas, or simply newer interpretations of a basic style, they all share certain characteristics, with some variation. More formal than not (without being necessarily

"grand"), they are ordered, geometric, and often symmetrical. Most are enclosed and intimate. Their organized structure reflects the needs and perspectives of a culture that prized order, balance, and economy.

The early settlers had a pragmatic approach to gardening, whether they were facing the harsh winters of Massachusetts or the milder climate of Virginia. First, it was essential to enclose each household compound to keep out animals, wild or domestic. Within a fence or stone wall was a well-planned setup that emphasized function, rather than aesthetics, without compromising overall harmony and charm. The location of the house, its outbuildings and connecting "yards," and planted areas were carefully sited for best drainage and exposure. Each had its specific purpose. Between the house and outbuildings was the "dooryard," where animals were shorn, soap made, or wool dyed. This rustic spot was hardly a place for much greenery, except for a few shade trees (which were also useful as places to attach pulleys to lift heavy objects).

Each family maintained a basic garden and orchard to serve its needs. These formal plantings were often wedged in small areas between the house, yards, sheds, barns, meadows, and pastures. At first, necessity dictated planting vegetables and fruit shrubs and trees, rather than flowers. (During the eighteenth century, gardens became less utilitarian and often included decorative plants, as well as edibles.) Orchards contained large fruit trees, such as apples, but pears, peaches, apricots, and plums were arranged in borders or espaliers closer to the house. Herbs used for cooking were planted in simple, rectangular plots next to the house, or were sometimes mixed in with other plants. Physicians sometimes kept a "physic garden," or botanic garden, to provide the proper curative herbs for their patients.

On large colonial southern plantations, it was especially essential to create kitchen gardens and orchards, as the plantations were often isolated from towns and villages. Unlike New England, plentiful varieties of English plants thrived there. According to Robert Beverly, who in 1705 wrote *History of the Present State of Virginia*, "A Kitchen-Garden don't thrive better or faster in any part of the Universe than there. They have all the Culinary Plants that grow in England, and in far greater perfection, than in England."

Most colonial gardens were arranged in neat, rectangular blocks bordered by boxwood (especially in the South) or other decorative plants. Separating these geometric, cultivated areas were brick or stone paths. The more elaborate gardens might also include a central azalea path aligned with the main door of the house and leading to a vista, stone bench, or statue. On either side of the walk were raised plots (for better drainage), usually arranged in symmetrical fashion. While vegetables and small fruits were kept in designated areas, ornamental plants surrounded the more important walkways. Sometimes edible plants and flowers were mixed in together, creating formal geometric designs.

In New England, especially in the more elegant houses of Boston and Providence, it was common practice to cultivate a garden in front of the house as well as in back. These tiny "parlor gardens" were sometimes no wider than the house itself and featured decorative shrubs and flowers.

During the eighteenth century, Philadelphia became one of the most important garden centers in the country. No doubt this was because of the Quakers' interest in botany and horticulture—not surprising in view of the fact that their austere lifestyle excluded most other arts and activities. The great horticulturist John Bartram, a Quaker who founded the first botanical garden in the colonies, was largely responsible for generating great interest in plants and gardens. The results of his efforts are still very evident in the historic colonial gardens found in the Philadelphia region.

In Virginia and other parts of the South, colonial gardens tended to be larger and more elaborate than in the North. With the large-scale introduction of slavery into the southern colonies, manor houses were built, surrounded by often grand landscaped settings. One such place is the Governor's Place in Williamsburg, reputed for its elegant eighteenth-century gardens (and a popular tourist attraction to this day). Another is Gunston Hall, an example of a well-designed twentieth-century re-creation featuring a stately arrangement of boxwoods growing in neat, geometric hedges.

Thomas Jefferson, who along with George Washington was one of the most famous colonial gardeners of all, had an abiding interest in horticulture, garden design, and botany—and a fundamental belief that the strength of the country lay in its agrarian society. He surrounded his extraordinary estate, Monticello, with vegetable plots (where he conducted various experiments), flower beds, and orchards. Monticello and Washington's Mount Vernon are examples of the colonial style at its grandest; but, still, they were created in basically the same spirit as the simplest colonial garden, emphasizing the order, harmony, and balance of pleasure and usefulness.

The Walled Garden

A Garden is my sister, my spouse; a spring shut up, a fountain sealed. Thy plants are an orchard of pomegranates with pleasant fruits.

— SONG OF SOLOMON

*T*HROUGHOUT HISTORY gardens have been seen as different, idealized worlds in which we create an orderly and beautiful environment cut off from tumultuous reality. Thus, of course, they must be enclosed. Most gardens, in fact, are surrounded in some way—separated from the wild, the urban, the public, the unknown. In this way gardens are like beautifully framed paintings. Such divisions between the wild and intrusive, and the cultivated and the private, create the sense of specialness and secrecy that characterizes an enclosed space. The "secret garden" is a concept that is undeniably inviting.

Artificial boundaries for gardens—when they are not naturally surrounded by geographical borders—are most often created by walls, hedges, or fences. Whether the border is formed by high boxwood hedges or medieval stone walls, trellis fences, or rows of evergreens, the "framing" of the garden is found all over the world, and throughout garden history.

The walled garden is the most private, for walls—whether of stone or hedge—can be high and impenetrable. Their origins are long in the past, when they kept out human and animal intruders and protected those within. In many cultures the enclosed garden, designed for both useful growing and pleasing contemplation, was a practical or an aesthetic choice. But the enclosed gardens of some civilizations—such as Egyptian and medieval Christian—were also metaphors for religious belief. (Walled gardens of the Middle Ages, for example, were thought to symbolize freedom and beauty with precisely set boundaries.)

Beautiful enclosed gardens can be seen in paintings from Egyptian and Roman walls, in Persian miniatures, and in the cloisters of medieval buildings. Trellis-fenced gardens appear in Renaissance art; the great classical gardens of France and England used both hedges and fences to enclose parts of their elaborate landscape designs. Boxwood, evergreen, and other living borders were common in gardens ranging from ancient Rome to colonial America, their carefully tended shapes creating dense hedgerows and geometric patterns.

Many of these garden boundaries were not just utilitarian borders to surround the plantings, but were integral parts of the garden design. Medieval walls featured carvings, patterned stonework, delicate espaliered trees or climbing plants, and carved stone blossoms reflecting the blooms within the garden. Some of the thick hedge borders of the most complex European gardens were cut into topiary designs, making the garden "walls" fantastic in shape and illusion.

American enclosed gardens date to colonial times, when their walls kept out the frightening wilderness. Many early American gardens have high brick walls and matching paths whose subtle deep red contrasts delightfully with the dark shiny greens of ivy and boxwood. Versions in the United States of European cloisters and Victorian "cottages" included walled gardens. Our great nineteenth-century estates include many enclosed garden areas, in which marble

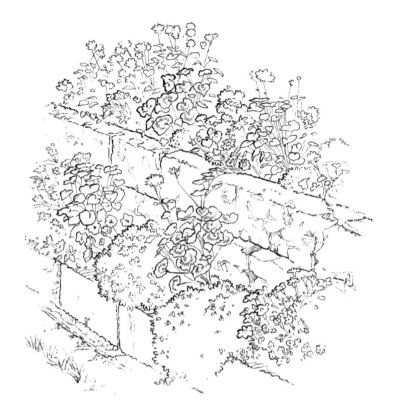

and granite not only provide a backdrop for plantings and sculpture, but create both color and texture in themselves. Espaliered fruit trees, climbing roses, ivies, wisteria, and trumpet vines are among the many popular plantings that can be seen covering the walls of enclosed gardens in New England.

Today the walled garden is often in the middle of a city. Urban gardeners use stone or brick walls in imaginative and contemporary ways, sometimes combining sculpture, falling water, and environmental design. Some of the smallest but most appealing walled gardens today are the "vest-pocket" parks in our cities.

Clearly, the concept of the enclosed garden is still valid; its plantings and design may be symbolic or practical or purely aesthetic, but the walled garden remains the special, magical space, serene and cut off from the world outside.

The Topiary Garden

And all these [flowers] by the skill of your Gardener, so comelily and orderly placed in your borders and squares and so intermingled, that one looking thereon, cannot but wonder to see, what Nature, corrected by Art, can do.

— WILLIAM LAWSON
A New Orchard and Garden, 1618

OPIARY, the ancient art of shaping plants into living sculptures, has brought charm, whimsy, and surprise to many a garden over the centuries. The term comes from the Latin *toparius*, referring to a gardener who specializes in carving plants; for it is such a gardener who, with the skill and vision of an artist, can transform an ordinary landscape into a delightful living tableau, adding both elegance and fun to the landscape. Because of its many possibilities of expression, topiary art has appealed to gardeners of all kinds, including the most eccentric, who find it an amusing outlet for their imaginations.

The topiary tradition comes with a wealth of sculpted plant shapes and designs. Shrubs and trees are pruned, clipped, cut, coaxed, and styled (sometimes on wire frames) into fanciful animals, mythological creatures, or elegant geometric forms. Yew, privet, hemlock, boxwood, and ivy—to name some of the most popular plants used—can be fashioned into peacocks, roosters, dragons, and centaurs, as well as pyramids, gloves, arches, and decorative scalloped hedges. Some topiary gardens feature entire sequential scenes: for example, a leafy foxhunt or a flotilla of ships. Others are created on an intimate scale and might include potted topiary that can be moved about or brought indoors.

Topiary gardens are not limited to green sculptures, however. There are also espalier gardens, knot gardens, parterres, and mazes. The espalier is a plant trained into an open, flat pattern to create a two-dimensional effect. The branches of shrubs and trees—often fruit trees such as pear, peach, and apple trees—are bent and pruned into intricate, delicate motifs to adorn walls and other vertical surfaces.

Knot gardens are level beds whose designs are made from the intertwining patterns of herbs and hedges. (Today's versions sometimes include flowers and pebbles as well.)

The parterre (French for "on the ground") is a variation of the knot garden. Usually on a larger scale, its designs are more fluid, with arabesques, open scrolls, or fleur-de-lis. Patterns are created by using carefully clipped dwarf hedges, flowers, grass, and colored stones.

The maze—one of the more delightful topiary forms—is like a lifesize puzzle. It is made of a network of connecting hedges and paths intended to amuse through surprise and confusion. In its earlier forms, in eighteenth-century Europe, the maze sometimes included hidden water games and sprays that were meant to catch the unsuspecting visitor by surprise, or well-hidden lovers' benches at the very center.

The history of topiary gardens shows us that though they were highly popular from Roman times until the eighteenth century, they are much more rare in contemporary gardens (though in European gardens of the past you will find many restored topiaries).

The earliest recorded topiary garden seems to have come about in ancient Rome. Around A.D. 100 the younger Pliny drew a distinction between the beauties of nature—beloved by the Romans—and the beauties of a cultivated garden. Pliny wrote long letters describing the gardens he had laid out at his Tuscan estate. Distinguishing between art and nature, he commented that the beauty of the landscape was owing to nature, while the beauty of his garden was owed to "art."

In describing in detail his plantings and garden design, Pliny indicated that his gardeners had employed what we know of today as topiary gardens. His paths, he wrote, were lined with boxwood hedges "and in between grass plots with box trees cut into all kinds of different shapes, some of them being letters spelling out the name of the owner or of the gardener who did the work." Interspersed with these topiary delights were white marble statues, obelisks, pillars, and seating areas.

A friend of emperor Augustus named C. Matius was responsible for the invention of the topiary garden. Matius, according to Pliny's uncle, had invented the cutting of trees into various shapes around 5 B.C. (Don't be surprised by the sophistication of ancient Roman gardeners; they had been grafting fruit trees, for example, for generations by the time Pliny made his gardens!)

We next hear of the topiary garden in medieval times, when the Flemish, in particular, favored small clipped evergreens (box or yew, as today) trained into tiers. (You can see a somewhat later example of the Flemish topiary in Pieter Brueghel's painting *Spring*.) But unlike the Romans, the Flemish apparently only clipped their evergreens in simple ways, rather than in the elaborate designs described by Pliny.

French medieval gardeners developed the espalier in their walled cities, where there was little room for orchards. The fact that espaliers required little space and that they bore their fruit early and abundantly was a great asset during those harsh times. Later espaliers became popular as purely ornamental features in French gardens.

(Also developed in France in the Middle Ages, by the way, were the first mazes: They were inspired by the medieval belief that a penitent soul might crawl on his hands and knees to imitate the path of earthly travail and thus gain heavenly grace.)

Topiary art came thoroughly into fashion in the Italian Renaissance, when all of the arts and their illusionary qualities were so admired, and when so many classical and ancient styles were revived. A "Renaissance" gentleman named Leon Battista Alberti described the principles of garden design in the fifteenth century. Among his many pieces of advice (on a wide range of architectural and landscaping subjects) was to select sites with "a view of cities, land and sea, a spreading plain, and the known peaks of the hills and mountains." He recommended cool shell-covered grottoes, groves of fruit trees, and box-bordered paths and topiary work. "The gardeners of ancient times," he said, "flattered their patrons by writing their names in letters formed in box and other odorous herbs." We can see examples of the elaborate gardens of the fifteenth and sixteenth centuries (such as those described by Alberti) in engravings and paintings from France and Italy and England.

In fact, in Queen Elizabeth the First's England of the sixteenth century, topiary designs, knot gardens, and mazes became quite fashionable at the palaces and castles of the aristocracy. At Sudely Castle in Gloucestershire, topiary yew hedges included small, doorlike openings for sheltering during England's sudden and frequent rainstorms, and Elizabeth's hunting lodge had both a knot garden and flat-cut hedges that are said to have been used for drying "linen, cloathes and yarne"! Among the designs used in Elizabethan gardens were "cockle shells," "beestes," "men armed in the field, ready to give battle," "swift-running grey-hounds," "pretty pyramides," and "little turrets with bellies." Later English gardens featured "outdoor rooms" in which the lawn was the carpet and the topiary the furniture.

France became a center of formal gardens under the Bourbon kings. In the seventeenth century, the art of topiary was apparently de rigueur in the great formal settings of the French châteaus. Extravaganzas of all kinds characterized French baroque court life; not the least of them were the elaborate pavilions and topiary designs. These included living plant decorations in the shapes of animals and people, sailing ships, and birds, as well as complex arrangements based on medieval dance patterns, parterres, three-part patterns, crisscrossed walks, mazes, and other features to entertain the lords and ladies who strolled through them.

But the craze for topiary gardens came to an end. In 1728 a French garden architect and writer (Alexandre Le Blond) wrote disparagingly, "At present nobody gives into these trifles [topiary gardens] in France, how well so ever they may be kept. . . . We chose rather a plain regularity less clutter'd and confus'd, which indeed looks much more noble and great." Rousseau's dedication to the principles of naturalism and informality and "the simple life" added to the dislike for the artificial topiary design. Instead a new emphasis on natural beauty replaced the intricate formal gardens of the baroque.

Visits to stately homes of Britain and châteaus of France will still often include historic topiary gardens and mazes. But in the United States, where we do not have the tradition in our past, they are more of a rarity. However, we have found several for your enjoyment. Read on!

The Conservatory Garden

> There is an inherent wonderful fascination in being able,
> in the middle of winter, to open the window of a salon
> and feel a balmy spring breeze instead of the raw Decem-
> ber or January air. It may be raining outside, or the snow
> may be falling in soft flakes from a black sky, but one
> opens the glass doors and finds oneself in an earthly para-
> dise that makes fun of the wintry showers.
> —Princess Mathilde de Bonaparte, 1869

THE IDEA OF collecting, nurturing, and displaying plants in an
enclosed, controlled environment is an ancient one. The first
greenhouses may have been built by the Romans to protect the

exotic plants they found during their military campaigns in distant lands. The emperor Nero's *specularium* (for so this type of Roman structure was called) contained his much loved cucumbers, which he could thus enjoy throughout the year. Over the course of human history, plants have been gathered, arranged, and housed for many reasons—from the most pragmatic to aesthetic, spiritual, scientific, or even whimsical. And their artificial habitats—from the specularium to the conservatory—have evolved considerably.

The earliest indoor gardens functioned both as places to display plants and to store and protect them from the sometimes harsh European winters. Ornamental plants were admired and often regarded as "trophies" won during victorious battles. (The taste for unusual flora existed at least as far back as ancient Egypt, when royal gardeners were routinely sent to other countries to gather rare species.) Crusaders and later many explorers came home with unfamiliar varieties, which required careful tending in controlled environments.

In sixteenth-century England and France, it became fashionable to maintain decorative citrus trees, and "orangeries" came into being. In the elegant estates of the time, these winter gardens were de rigueur. During the coldest months, orange and lemon trees in large tubs were placed in neat rows inside glass-walled chambers, mostly for show. Some were on a very grand scale; indeed, the 9,000-square-foot orangerie at Heidelberg Castle in 1619 included more than 400 trees, many of which were at least 25 feet high!

But the real "botanic" gardens filled with rare plants—both indoor and outdoor—came into being as a result of a new interest in the spiritual and scientific dimensions of the plant kingdom. The garden of Eden was actually the inspiration for the botanic gardens of the sixteenth century. After the discovery of the New World's natural life, the first notion arose of a *hortus inculsis*, a gathering of all the plants that had been dispersed from that Biblical paradise.

Exotic plants brought back from voyages around the world formed the basis for the first botanic gardens at Leiden, Padua, and Montpellier. In the next century, others were started in Paris, London, and Uppsala, Sweden.

Most of these early gardens were arranged in squares, divided into quadrants representing the four corners of the earth (in those days that meant Asia, Africa, Europe, and America). The quadrants were then divided into parterres, with grass walks dividing them. Each plant was carefully labeled; the botanic garden became a "living encyclopedia" of Creation. (It was believed, in fact, that the visitor who spent time contemplating in such a place might regain his or her lost innocence and even gain insight into the "mind of God.")

By the seventeenth century, theologians upset this easy method of finding paradise. (They looked at zoos—established for the same reason—and saw no peaceable kngdoms ensuing.) Some great thinkers believed that the natural wilderness was closer to the original than these highly organized settings. And there were problems of a more practical nature: Which climate did the garden of Eden have? Plants from so many different climes could not grow in the same place at the same temperature. The botanic garden as a place of science was created; it featured indoor and outdoor areas devoted to climactic differences, propagation, and the survival of species.

In their capacity as "laboratories" for scientific study, botanic gardens and, particularly, greenhouses, became places to grow plants for medicinal purposes. During the seventeenth and eighteenth centuries, botanists traveled to the New World on merchant ships to identify and gather species of possible medicinal or other scientific value. John Bartram, among the most famous of these botanists, discovered many valuable tropical plants in his scientific expeditions abroad. (He was, by the way, a member of Capt. James Cook's scientific expedition in 1772.)

The emphasis on greenhouses and imported rarities from all

over the world also had an artistic effect: the concept of a "museum" of plants. The early botanic garden became a collection of exotic and fascinating individual plants, set out for easy enjoyment and identification, rather than a larger, overall form of environmental or artistic beauty. (As we will see, these diverse aims have been admirably united in the botanic gardens of today.)

One of the first great botanical gardens in the United States was in New York City, where Rockefeller Center is today; the Elgin Botanic Garden was started in 1801. A huge area with a conservatory featured scientifically identified plants. The garden—then in "the wilds" of upper Manhattan—was surrounded by a belt of trees and a great stone wall. Needless to say, it did not survive the city's expansion.

But in 1824 a Belgian horticulturalist named André Parmentier came to New York and built the Brooklyn Botanic Garden. One of its most popular aspects was a tower from which visitors could see the gardens and surrounding area with a bird's-eye view. Parmentier's wonderful gardens still exist today and can be visited.

Another such enterprise was begun only twenty-nine years after Washington, D.C., became the capital of the United States (in 1820), when a group of amateur scientists founded a similar enterprise there. Although the garden lasted for only about eighteen years before it ran out of funds, the idea of a national botanic garden was taken up again in 1842.

Plans for a new garden were encouraged by the 1838–42 commercial expedition of Capt. Charles Wilkes (the model for Captain Ahab, by the way). He had circumnavigated the globe with 440 men and six ships (one of which must have been needed just to carry home the 10,000 plant variety seeds, dried samples, and live plants he collected from all over the world!). A federally funded national botanic garden was finally built in 1842. In 1849 it was moved to its present location and it can be visited today in all its splendor.

As indoor gardens have had a variety of functions over the ages, so too have they evolved stylistically. The earliest greenhouses contained little glass; indeed, it is likely that Romans used sheets of mica instead to allow the sun to filter in. With improved technology, particularly during the industrial age, greenhouses became all-glass structures and took on new shapes. While eighteenth-century orangeries and conservatories had had extensive windows but conventional roofs, in the nineteenth century they began to be built with domed roofs. Theorists had discovered that the form of roof best suited for the admission of the sun's rays was hemispherical. Because of the development of iron frames and glazed roofs, it was now possible to build greenhouses that looked like what we now think of as "conservatories" (and what we imagine when we inevitably read about them in Victorian novels). These elegant and fanciful structures culminated with Sir Joseph Paxton's famous Crystal Palace, inaugurated as the main attraction at the First International Exhibition in London's Hyde Park in 1851. Greeted with great enthusiasm, its enormous success helped stimulate the building of conservatories everywhere, including in America. More elaborate than greenhouses, conservatories contained plants primarily chosen for their showy effect.

The Water Garden

> Any garden ornament or piece of architecture mirrored in water receives an addition to its dignity by the repetition and continuation of upright line.
>
> —GERTRUDE JEKYLL, 1901

WATER HAS embellished gardens around the world since the earliest civilizations. It has been used in gardens not only for practical reasons but also for pure pleasure and decoration. The effects of water on the senses are varied and fascinating: Water can delight, charm, soothe, cool, stimulate, and excite. Through its magical powers of illusion, and reflection, it can create an environment of mystery and even surprise. Natural sources of water—streams, brooks, or waterfalls—as well as artful canals, pools, or fountains have been focal points in gardens over the ages.

The Egyptians were among the first who recognized the importance of "decorative water" in garden design. Ancient tomb paintings depict gardens with rectangular pools, lilies, lotus, and papyrus. Not only were these basins of water practical—they were used to irrigate the surroundings—but they were also refreshingly appealing in the parched lands.

The pleasure-loving Romans copied these early models in their own gardens, adding more sophisticated elements, such as elaborate fountains and canals. The fabled garden of Pliny the Younger included (according to his nephew) "a semicircular bench of white marble shaded with a vine which is trained on four small pillars of marble. Water, gushing through several little pipes from under this bench . . . falls onto a stone cistern underneath, from whence it is

received into a fine polished marble basin, so artfully contrived that it is always full without overflowing." It seems that at mealtime, plates of food were placed on the water so they could float from one person to the next.

Water, revered by the Persians as the essence of life, was the chief element in their paradise gardens. These magnificent, enclosed oases with fountains, tiled pools, and intricate water channels provided a delicious respite in a torrid climate. Formal and geometric, they usually included rows of stately cypress trees and scented roses, irrigated by underground tunnels.

Water gardens reached some of their highest levels of artistry in those created by the Moors of medieval Spain. Such magnificent and lavish gardens as those in the Alhambra were intricately planned by some of the most sophisticated designers of all time. These masterful hydraulic engineers/artists used ingenious techniques to channel precious water from distant mountain springs through elaborate tunnels to palaces and courtyards. The gardens were thus filled with the sight and sound of water continuously flowing (and recycled) through fountains, marbled channels, and basins.

The rest of Europe (which during the Middle Ages had confined its gardens to relatively modest cloisters with small wells and fountains) saw a rebirth of the water garden during the Renaissance, especially in Italy. Along with a renewed interest in antiquities came a fascination with science and the study of such basic elements as water; water became a central focus of Italian villa gardens. Amidst the waters of elegant fountains and graceful pools, and even inside mysterious grottoes, Italian designers placed statues depicting mythological characters—ranging from river gods and gorgons to Venus and Neptune surrounded by nymphs and dolphins. Amazing waterpowered machines and animated ornaments graced some villa gardens. The fabled Villa d'Este, one of the most dazzling water gardens of all time (it still delights visitors today), displayed spectacular aquatic fireworks in addition to its other exquisite garden features.

Fountains were used most lavishly in seventeenth-century French gardens. At Versailles, for example, the master designer André Le Nôtre (along with an army of artists and engineers) channeled water through myriad dams, falls, pools, cascades, and an especially long canal (where mock naval battles were occasionally held to amuse the courtiers). Le Nôtre's designs for Versailles became a standard by which numerous other formal gardens were (and are still) measured.

Romantic English gardens used water in a less artificial way. Instead of the grand geometric, formal pools, and fountains of the French, they featured meandering streams and rivers surrounded with naturalistic plantings and graceful garden paths. Some of the great Capability Brown's designs called for picturesque garden lakes, created by dammed streams and massive excavations.

Of course, the "natural" use of water—so favored in the romantic era—had long been featured in the gardens of the Far East. In classical Chinese and Japanese gardens, water, regarded as a vital ingredient, appeared almost always in an entirely naturalistic way. But water in Asian gardens also had symbolic significance; for example, both the sight and the sound of water in Japanese gardens is part of the aesthetic importance of their traditional gardens. (See the remarks about Asian gardens.)

Today water gardens have been inspired by these varied historic and cultural traditions and reinterpreted to accommodate contemporary needs and tastes. As you visit gardens that feature water designs, you will perhaps identify some of these stylistic elements.

The Rock Garden

> It may appear at first that the collection of stones etc. is designed to appear wild and irregular, little Art would be required in its construction; but this is so far from being the case, that perhaps rockwork is more difficult to design and execute than any other kind of garden scenery.
>
> —JANE LOUDON, CA. 1930

WE TAKE rock gardens for granted nowadays, enjoying the combination of hard, surprising stone and delicate, careful plantings. Many a rocky American hillside is planted these days with wildflowers and alpine specialties, and some such gardens are even created from the start.

But the rock garden does not have as long a history as most of the designs and styles of gardens we describe. In fact, the rock garden dates to 1777, when Sir Joseph Banks, a British naturalist (and president of the Royal Society some years later), visited Iceland. On

a twelve-day hike to a volcanic mountain in Iceland, Banks collected the lava from the volcano's last eruption five years earlier. (He used it for ballast for his ship on the return to Britain.)

When he got home, he presented the hardened lava to the Chelsea Physic Garden, where it was combined with piles of stone from the old walls of the Tower of London, discarded bricks, and various other types of stone. Plants began to grow all over this huge and motley mound of rock.

Within fifty years, rock gardens were popular in Britain. Jane and John Loudon, noted writers on all subjects of gardening, described "rockwork" as fragments of rock "thrown together in an artistic manner, so as to produce a striking and pleasing effect, and to serve as a nest or repository" for a variety of plants. Rock gardens are more difficult to design than they look, they warned their readers. As the "cluttered" garden (much like the Victorian parlor) soon replaced the expansive, airy stretches of the previous era, the rock garden with its many composite parts became more and more popular.

Among the early designs in private gardens for rockeries, as they were known, were an imitation Swiss mountain scene made of white marble to simulate snow, and a naturalistic rocky hollow made from an abandoned quarry. Plants for these original gardens varied from traditional British ornamental shrubs and flowers to imported specimens, originating from rocky hillsides in other countries.

By midcentury many English rock gardens were devoted entirely to alpine plants in the Swiss style, even though the plants' native habitat on high, snowy mountains could not easily be transplanted to Britain. Advice proliferated on caring for such plants—described as "low, bushy, and evergreen" and "tiny and elfin"—and on how to design the rockeries. Before long, the rock garden became synonymous with the alpine garden and a fashionable addition to many a country estate, where miniature mountains, gorges, valleys, waterfalls, and bridges appeared.

The alpine garden was the subject of intense interest to botanists and gardeners who traveled the world in search of rare plants that adapted well to their stony surroundings. The designs for such gardens were described by Reginald Farrer in *My Rock Garden*. He wrote derisively that there were three common ideas for rock gardens: the "Almond Pudding scheme," which has spiky pinnacles of limestone jutting up among the plants; the "Dog's Grave," with a pudding shape but its stones laid flat; and the "Devil's Lapful," which contains cartloads of bald, square-faced boulders dropped about anywhere, with plants dropped in between them. He preferred a naturalistic setting. (And so did many later garden designers, who went so far as to use imitation rocks to create "lifelike" landscapes.)

Today the alpine idea is still popular, but it is no longer an imitative or confining design. There is great freedom of idea and layout in the American rock gardens we have visited. Many combine the naturalistic features of a rocky terrain (with the huge boulders common to our part of the world) and a judicious use of stone walls and stairways and other rocky additions. The plantings in these gardens range widely from imported alpine delicacies to plants that lend themselves to falling over stone walls. Raised beds, stone pools, and tiny waterfalls are among the elements you might find.

The Asian Garden

> A lonely pond in age-old stillness sleeps,
> Apart, unstirred by sound or motion till
> Suddenly into it a little frog leaps . . .
>
> —BASHO (1644–94)

GARDENS OF the Orient were the first to become living artistic statements. Closely aligned with religious beliefs of Buddhism, Taoism, and Shintoism, Chinese and Japanese gardens were places

of meditation and renewal. In an attempt to tame nature's wildness, deliberately placed trees and plants were combined with materials of long-lasting value, like wood, sand, and stone. Each element of the garden was symbolic, designed for spiritual awareness as its owners strolled through it.

Chinese "cup gardens"—ranging in size from picturesque lakes surrounded by hills to small stone areas with a bonsai (artificially pruned, miniature tree) in the center—were among the first symbolically designed Asian gardens. The earliest cup garden is believed to have been created by the great landscape painter and poet Wang Wei (A.D. 699–759) during the T'ang dynasty. It was Wang Wei who first articulated the close relationship of the Chinese garden to art, poetry, and spirituality.

If you look at a traditional scroll painting of a Chinese landscape, in fact, it is hard to know which art is imitating which. For the great Chinese gardens have the ambience of paintings, while the paintings seem inextricably bound up with the delicately designed traditional garden. Harmonious in design, the Chinese landscape is distinctive, with its careful balance of leaning trees and craggy rocks, arched bridges over reflective water, and gentle flowering plants.

The cup garden was surrounded (like the inside of a cup) by a wall, hedge, or other barrier in order to provide isolation from the chaos of the outside world. Within its boundaries, the cup garden drew the visitor's attention to accents—a particular plant or stone or body of water. The garden's purpose was introspection and privacy, using an artistic design and symbolism to bring close communication and union with nature and its forces.

The symbolic elements and design of ancient Chinese gardens strongly influenced the Japanese, who went on to create elaborate and exquisite gardens of their own. The Japanese stroll garden also became a place for introspection: an orderly, aesthetic environment where balance, beauty, and harmony mirrored the proper harmony of the soul.

There is little that is accidental or uncalculated in a Japanese garden. Carefully placed, asymmetrical plantings—such as bamboo and katsura trees, ferns, delicate iris, or lilies—grow among symbolic settings. These important elements range from free-form ponds that reflect the sky, to statuary such as small deities or cranes (representing wisdom and long life), to raked sand (representing the ocean's tides), to carefully placed rocks and small stones (suggesting the earth's natural forms), to tiny islands in the pond (symbolizing clouds). Small buildings such as the familiar Japanese teahouse provide a haven of peace and beauty. To the Shintoists, spirits inhabit all natural phenomena, and the Japanese garden suggests no less than heaven on earth.

Southeast Asian gardens share many of the same designs and ideas, but in Thailand and Burma, for example, there is greater freedom from the precise symbolism of the Japanese. Though not as burdened by the meaning of each rock and bamboo shoot, these gardens are also spiritual sanctuaries adorned with sculptured deities, including small Buddhas set amid the greenery and flowers.

The Asian garden stunned and delighted Westerners who traveled to the East. In the seventeenth and eighteenth centuries, many aspects of Chinese artistry—including garden design and exotic plants—began to appear in European gardens and subsequently in America.

Today, in addition to many great Chinese and Japanese gardens carefully maintained in the United States, we also find Oriental plantings and landscape design intermixed with the more Western styles of many of our American gardens. Among the elements adopted in our own gardens are numerous exotic trees (ranging from Asian magnolias and rhododendrons to Japanese flowering cherries) and many flowers, including species of jasmine, poppies, azaleas, and lilies.

But even more obvious to our Western eyes are the elements of Asian design that have crept into our own formal and informal gardens: trickling water and delicate lily ponds, small arched bridges and waterfalls, "living still lifes of stones and foliage so prized in Asian design, and garden areas created for meditation and harmony with nature."

Gardenwalks in Connecticut

*T*here is a competition between nature and art, and what one fails in the other produces, is one of the first allusions to horticultural work as an "art" form.

—WILLIAM OF MALMESBURY, twelfth century

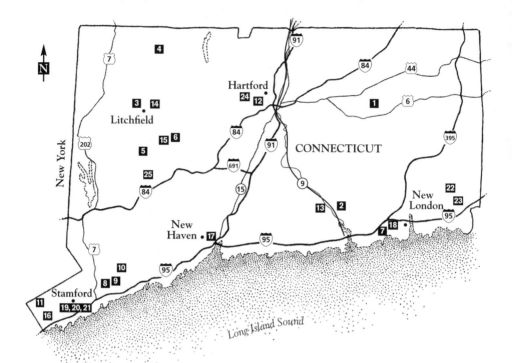

1. Coventry: Caprilands Herb Farm
2. East Haddam: Gillette Castle State Park
3. Litchfield: Laurel Ridge Foundation
4. Norfolk: Hillside Gardens
5. North Bethlehem: Bellamy-Ferriday Garden
6. Thomaston: Cricket Hill Garden
7. Waterford: Harkness Memorial State Park
8. Westport: Private Garden of Susan and Robert Beeby

Don't Miss . . .

9. Fairfield: Larsen Sanctuary of Connecticut Audubon Society
10. Fairfield: Ogden House and Gardens
11. Greenwich: Fairchild Connecticut Wildflower Gardens

12. Hartford: Nook Farm
13. Higganum: Sundial Herb Gardens
14. Litchfield: Topsmead State Forest
15. Morris: White Flower Farm
16. New Canaan: Olive W. Lee Memorial Garden
17. New Haven: Edgerton Park
18. New London: Connecticut College Arboretum
19. Stamford: Bartlett Arboretum
20. Stamford: Old Fort Stamford
21. Stamford: Stamford Museum and Nature Center
22. Stonington: Adam's Garden of Eden
23. Stonington: Stonington Vineyards
24. West Hartford: Elizabeth Park
25. Woodbury: Gertrude Jekyll Garden at the Glebe House Museum

1. Caprilands Herb Farm

5334 Silver Street, **Coventry,** CT
(860) 742-7244, www.caprilands.com

$\mathcal{O}$NE OF THE MOST enjoyable types of gardens to visit is the eccentric garden. Occasionally people see their gardens as canvases or notebooks in which to present their own visions of color and composition, as well as personal meaning. Such thematic gardens express their owners' views and personalities; sometimes we are lucky enough to find a variety of themes all in one large, very personal garden.

Caprilands Herb Farm is one such place. It was the creation of the redoubtable Adelma Simmons, who for more than sixty years guided its unusual path. On what was once a rock-strewn Connecticut dairy farm (bought by her family in 1929), Miss Simmons built an irregular series of separate gardens with whimsical names and intriguing quotations propped among the flowers. Typical low stone walls divide the fifty-acre landscape. Primarily an herb farm growing some 360 varieties of herbs, Caprilands also includes any number of flowers and shrubs (and weeds too). There is nothing pristine nor formal about this landscape—in fact, that is part of its great charm.

While Caprilands began as a venture in growing and selling herbs to the public (and still has a shop in a barn, a large mail-order business, a lecture series, a basket shop, a lunch, high tea in the colonial-style farmhouse, and clients for its herbs—including such noted chefs as Pierre Bouley), there is little that seems tastelessly commercial here. Instead, the visitor ambles through overgrown paths, seeking the various thematic gardens as identified on old school slates. Bits of wood and statuary adorn the pocket-size gardens. A map is available at the desk.

Each separate bed has a name and a theme illustrated by the flowers or herbs chosen by Miss Simmons. She used to spend each long day, except for a few holidays, overseeing the gardening and regally receiving curious and admiring visitors from her chair in the shop in the weathered barn (formerly the milk house). There you can purchase herbs and her books—some fifty different titles, including her best-known *Herb Gardening in Five Seasons*.

Among the thirty thematic gardens that caught our attention were the Medieval Garden (in which all the flowers and leaves are silver), the Garden of the Stars (in which plantings are divided into twelve culinary beds based on signs of the zodiac), the Saints' Garden (adorned with small statuary and planted with symbolic plants such as rosemary and Madonna lilies), the Shakespeare Garden (with appropriate quotations), the Bride's Garden (in which two hearts outlined in brick are filled with symbolic plants representing love

throughout history—lemon verbena, forget-me-nots, orange trees), and more practical gardens like the Cook's Garden and the Salad Garden. There are plots devoted to colors—gold, blue, white—and there are gardens for dyeing colors, for potpourri, for flowers that are good for drying or for fragrance, and even for onions.

Most of these small, patterned beds are delightful in their own miniature way. (For the serious visitor, a guidebook by Adelma Simmons—who was exceptionally knowledgeable about the history and herbal uses for each plant—is available. It identifies the plants and describes the symbolism, preservation, and practical use of each.) For those who prefer the literary reference, handwritten quotations abound.

About tansy (*Tanacetum*): "On Easter Sunday be the pudding seen / To which tansy lends her sober green" (from the *Oxford Sausage*).

About onions: "This is every cook's opinion, / no savory dish without an onion, / But lest your kissing should be spoiled / Your onions must be fully foiled" (by John Swift).

About broom: "I'm sent with Broom before / To sweep the dust behind the door" (Shakespeare, in *Midsummer Night's Dream*).

Caprilands is a particularly interesting garden visit for young naturalists, because here they can wander on their own with map or guide in hand and search out hundreds of different plants. The historic, medicinal, and culinary uses are truly fascinating. And for those of us who simply enjoy the color and variety of unusual and surprising plantings, Caprilands is made for exploring.

❁ **Admission:** Fee.

Garden open: Daily except major holidays. We recommend a visit in spring or summer. (In the winter it is open only in the afternoons.)

Further information: There are numerous special events, including lectures and demonstrations of herbal uses. Call for details.

Directions: Caprilands Herb Farm is located just off Route 44. From Hartford take Interstate 84 East to exit 59, which is Interstate 384. Go to its end and turn left onto Route 44 east. Silver Street is a right-hand exit from Route 44.

2. Gillette Castle State Park

East Haddam, CT, (860) 526-2336, www.friendsofgillettecastle.org

*G*ILLETTE CASTLE is a celebration of eccentricity. Perched high atop one of seven hills (known as the Seven Sisters) overlooking the scenic Connecticut River—and surrounded by 122 acres of woodland—it appears as a grandiose folly from a bygone era. The craggy, hand-built fieldstone castle, terraced gardens, high walls, and woodsy pathways connected by suspended bridges and the remnants of a private outdoor railroad—trestles, tunnels, and all— paint a picture of unusual imagination and whimsy. The fact that the castle is also accessible by ferry—a delightful five-minute boat ride to the east side of the river—adds a touch of romance to this adventure.

The creator of this unique site was William Hooker Gillette, a longtime actor and playwright whose portrayal of Sherlock Holmes had finally brought him fame. In 1913, while looking for the ideal place to build his dream home, he was captivated by this picturesque riverfront location with its sweeping views. Naming the property Seventh Sister after the southernmost hill of the region, he began a most ambitious construction project.

Gillette himself designed the twenty-four-room castle, its thick, fortresslike granite walls, and its eclectic interior. He personally supervised the intricate hand-hewn woodwork, stone carvings, and other decorative details. Using his lively imagination and sense of fun, he came up with fanciful ideas—such as making each of the forty-seven oak doors different from one another, or hanging lighting fixtures with garlands of colored glass salvaged from old bottles, or fashioning doorstops and mantels in catlike shapes. (A lover of cats, he is at one time supposed to have kept fifteen on the premises.) It took about five years for his army of twenty-five workers to complete construction—and well over a million dollars (an extraordinarily impressive sum at the time).

This nonconformist who, according to his contemporaries, had "uncanny inventive ability, a precocious and daring initiative, and a total disregard for accepted standards and ways," took a great delight in developing the grounds surrounding his castle. A train and locomotive enthusiast, he built for himself and his friends a man-size railroad that began at the castle and wound around through the forest, making a 3-mile loop. (Although the railroad has since been dismantled, signs of it remain.) He also created intricate walking paths and constructed giant vertical steps, arched stone bridges, wooden trestles, and a goldfish pond. (Many of these oddities can still be found.) The gardens here are just one part of an eccentric and always interesting landscape.

Gillette's will stipulated that the property should not "fall into the hands of some blithering saphead who has no conception of where he is or with what surrounded." Accordingly, after his death the property was acquired by the state. In 1943 Gillette Castle State Park was officially created, and it has attracted thousands of visitors over the years.

Anyone—old and young alike—will be enchanted by this intriguing site. Children will be fascinated by the looming medieval-like fortress, the old railroad beds, and the many woodsy paths to be explored. There are wonderful hiking trails for those so inclined. Garden lovers and others sensitive to nature's beauties will find the extraordinary views and setting inspiring. Unlike many other grand estates, the castle does not include traditional formal gardens (nothing is "conventional" about this place); it does have, however, unusually inviting terrace gardens and a beautifully maintained conservatory. The terraces, graced by charming flower beds and other contained plantings, offer the most spectacular river and hillside views of all. You will want to linger in these "gardens with a view."

For an entrance fee, you can visit the castle and enjoy its many eccentricities either by guided tour or on your own. On the other hand, you are free to roam the vast grounds, including the terrace gardens, at will perhaps enjoying a picnic at the end of your explorations. Gillette Castle is best seen off-season, perhaps on a bright day in early fall, when you might have the place almost to yourself, including the ferryboat.

✿ **Admission:** Fee for the castle only.

Garden open: Gillette Castle State Park is open daily 8:00 A.M. to sunset. The castle is open 10:00 A.M. to 5:00 P.M. from Memorial Day to Columbus Day, and weekends only 10:00 A.M. to 4:00 P.M. from Columbus Day to the last weekend before Christmas.

Further information: The Chester–Hadlyme car ferry operates from early morning until sunset, for a fee, from April through November. Alternatively, you can reach the castle via a more roundabout road and bridge. After your visit, don't miss the charming nearby village of Chester. You will enjoy its elegant shops and sidewalk cafes.

Directions: From Interstate 95 go north on Route 9 (near Old Saybrook) to Route 148 east, past Chester. Follow signs to the ferry. As you cross the river, you will see the castle directly in front of you, its unmistakable silhouette looming above.

3. Laurel Ridge Foundation

Wigwam Road, **Litchfield,** CT

*L*AUREL RIDGE is without doubt one of the most enchanting and unspoiled spots we have discovered in our many garden ramblings. To reach this little-known hillside narcissus garden, you pass through some of northwestern Connecticut's most picturesque countryside of rolling hills, winding roads, stone walls, and ponds. Along the way, you even see a working windmill, something of a rarity these days.

The site itself is an open and free and wild landscape, rather than a traditional garden. Some ten bucolic acres of gently sloping woodland, fields, and wonderfully aged stone walls overlook a small sparkling lake with two tiny islands. Literally covering the hillside

—and on one of the islands—are thousands and thousands of daffodils growing at random, swaying in the soft breezes. In late April and early May, this spectacular sight truly takes your breath away.

At Laurel Ridge there are none of the usual signs of a public garden—no gates, admission fees, gift shops, or crowds; a small, discrete sign merely indicates the site and asks you not to bring in dogs. After leaving your car by the side of the road, you are on your own to wander about freely, from dawn to dusk. Some rustic stone steps invite you to walk down the slope to simple, meandering paths (created by walkers) leading you up and down and around the lake and beyond. This is a quiet place, where you can enjoy the sounds of nature and have the place practically to yourself.

The first narcissus display was planted in 1941. Over the years the original ten thousand daffodils have naturalized and multiplied. The current owners of the property (who live across the road and up a hill) fortunately have maintained the display, adding thousands of new plants every year—and have very generously shared their exceptional garden with the public. The different varieties create three distinctive color peaks: in late April the overall color scheme is a dark yellow, followed by a softer yellow and, finally, a dreamy white in mid-May.

You will want to linger at Laurel Ridge, perhaps even picnic at a spot of your own choosing (picnicking is allowed, so long as you make sure not to leave anything behind).

❀ **Admission:** Free.

Garden open: Daily from dawn to dusk.

Further information: Plan to visit in late April or during the first two weeks of May, when the daffodils are at their full glory. There is no telephone number.

Directions: Laurel Ridge is a few miles from the center of Litchfield. From Litchfield village take Route 118 east to Route 254 for 3 miles. Turn right onto Wigwam Road. Laurel Ridge is located about 1 mile on the left.

4. Hillside Gardens

515 Litchfield Road, **Norfolk,** CT, (860) 542–5345

*H*ILLSIDE GARDENS, in the heart of northwest Connecticut's rural back roads, is a pleasant combination of perennial display gardens and nursery. Situated on five acres surrounding the colonial farmhouse of the owners Fred and Mary Ann McGourty, the site adjoins a state park, which boasts some of the most scenic vistas in the state. This is not your typical commercial nursery—indeed, it is barely noticeable from the road. The ambience is more that of a country garden than anything else. Plants are arranged in natural-looking borders rather than in standard nursery rows. The gently sloped land has beautiful old stone walls, a 600-foot-long berm, fields, and woods.

Hillside is one of the few private residential gardens in the region that welcome visitors on a regular basis. Whether or not you intend to buy from its wide and unusual assortment of perennials, you are free to wander about amid the lovely plantings, or consult with the staff on garden questions.

Cultivating this northern site, whose elevation rises to some 1,400 feet, is quite a challenge. Only hardy plants seem to thrive, and the growing season is relatively short. But from May through September, the rapid succession of blossoming perennials makes the gardens a delight, particularly during their late July peak. From the first daffodils, primulas, colombines, irises, and peonies of spring, to summer's phloxes, daylilies, foxgloves, and Russian sage, to September's asters, chrysanthemums, and elegant ornamental grasses, Hillside is a changing tableau of colors.

You will find a visit to Hillside an informative and pleasant experience, which you might wish to combine with a nature walk and picnic in the nearby preserve.

✿ **Admission:** Free if you walk about on your own; guided tours are available (for a fee) by previous arrangement.

Garden open: Daily 9:00 A.M. to 5:00 P.M., except holidays, from May 1 to September 15.

Further information: Hillside Gardens is located at Route 272 in Norfolk, 11 miles north of Torrington.

Directions: From New York: Take Interstate 684 east to I–84 to Waterbury. Go north on Route 8 to Route 4 in Torrington. Take Route 4 to Route 272 and follow Route 272 north for about 11 miles, then look for a small sign. The gardens are on your right and parking on your left.

5. Bellamy-Ferriday Garden

9 Main Street, **North Bethlehem,** CT, (203) 266-7596
www.ci.bethlehem.ct.us/Bellamy/bellamy.htm

*T*HE BELLAMY-FERRIDAY ESTATE combines the best of a Connecticut landscape with a delightful semiformal garden. The mansion and numerous farm buildings (open to the public) sit serenely in their green and rolling landscape of gently sloping fields divided by stone walls, flowering trees, and quiet woods. The nine-acre estate is now contiguous to a much larger preserved forest area for hiking.

The original house was built in 1744 by Joseph Bellamy, the local pastor and director of the first divinity school in America. (He was also known as "the Pope of Litchfield County" for his theological tract called *True Religion Delineated*). His son and heirs and subsequent owners added to the building, making it the fine mansion of today with a Palladian facade, verandas, and great windows. Long a working farm, the estate's simple white eighteenth- and nineteenth-century outbuildings (including an old schoolhouse) are clustered nearby. In 1912 the Ferriday family bought the farm. Mrs. Ferriday and her daughter not only added to the house, but also reshaped the landscape and planted the charming garden that has been restored today.

It was Mrs. Ferriday who put in the great lawn, planted the wall of evergreens that now shield the house from the road, and tended the orchard (first planted in 1750), lilacs, peonies, roses, and specimen trees. Her daughter, Caroline, further restored the house and grounds and prepared the estate for preservation. She assured its future by bequeathing it to the Antiquarian and Landmarks Society, who have continued the restoration. Today you'll find a colorful collection of blooming shrubs (magnolias, Japanese snowballs, lilacs, and peonies, among others) all over the property. (A map is available at the desk.)

Of particular interest to garden lovers, of course, is the formal garden and rose collection. First designed in 1920, this exceptionally pretty arrangement is next to the house in a sheltered and invitingly terraced and enclosed area. Here in unusual serpentine, yew-edged planting beds are a heady mix of flowers—an informal profusion within formal outlines. A small circular pool with stone edges and a statue add to the romantic aura of this intimate garden.

We found this to be one of the most pleasing gardens we have seen—one certainly to inspire the home gardener, for it is neither of grand size nor exotic in plantings. It is, instead, particularly well conceived, with an unusual eye for color and ambience. The use of local stones for walls and terraces adds to its harmonious setting within the larger landscape.

❀ **Admission:** Fee.

Garden open: Wednesday, Saturday, and Sunday 11:00 A.M. to 4:00 P.M. from May through October.

Further information: There are a number of special events supporting the restoration. Hiking trails are accessible from the property.

Directions: The Bellamy-Ferriday Garden is north of Bethlehem. From I–84 in Connecticut, take Route 6 north to Route 61 north; Bethlehem is at the intersection of Routes 61 and 132 (south of Litchfield).

6. Cricket Hill Garden

670 Walnut Hill Road, **Thomaston,** CT, (860) 283–1042
www.treepeony.com

CRICKET HILL GARDEN could well be subtitled "Peony Heaven" (in fact, the very name of one of its publications), so glorious is its peony collection—and so idyllic. Overlooking a pond, meadows, and woodlands in the picturesque Connecticut highlands, this low-key, rural nursery/display garden can't help but appeal to those sensitive to nature's beauties, whether or not they have a particular love for the peony. What makes Cricket Hill extra special is that it features the Chinese tree peony, a more unusual variety that has inspired Chinese artists and poets since ancient times.

Ideally, you should plan to visit during the last two weeks in May, when the glorious blossoms are at their peak. You will be treated to a blissfully colorful and fragrant tableau of tree peonies interspersed with tulips and other plantings, set on three acres of gently sloped, terraced hillside. These peonies (some one hundred varieties, we are told) are quite different from the more widely known herbaceous type that is often found in old-fashioned gardens. Ranging in height between 4 to 10 feet when fully grown, they have woody, shrublike stems and generously proportioned leaves. The blossoms (measuring 6 to 12 inches in diameter) form an assortment of cylindrical or rounded shapes, sometimes on the very same plant. The flowers come in the most subtle shades of violet, pink, magenta, yellow, gold, or cream. Tree peonies can live to be quite old, some even reaching one hundred (although there are none of this vintage in this relatively new site). Unlike the common herbaceous peonies, they continue to grow from one season to the next and don't simply vanish during the winter months.

Not surprisingly, the owners, creators, and gardeners of Cricket Hill, Kasha and David Furman, are passionate advocates of the

Chinese tree peony. They publish valuable information (readily available) on the subject ranging from a journal to sundry catalogs— and are eager to share their vast knowledge with any willing listener. Topics might include anything from such practical matters as the ideal soil, sun exposure, or suitable climate for cultivating the tree peony, to the plant's long history and its importance in traditional Chinese culture.

Records of this most renowned flowering plant of ancient China date as far back as the fourth century A.D. Revered for its extraordinary fragrance and abundant blossoms, the tree peony was grown in profusion in the imperial gardens. It was admired by much of society, including the nobility, who would routinely travel great distances with horse and carriage to view it in its many variations. The *mudan*—its name in Chinese—was also a great source of inspiration for poets and painters, as the many traditional painted scrolls attest.

During the T'ang dynasty, the mudan reached its peak of popularity and graced many gardens. Considered a representation of sensual beauty and wealth, it became the only flower to gain a permanent place in the traditional Chinese garden, along with rocks, water, and trees. In China today you can still find stands of mudan that are hundreds of years old.

The Chinese tree peonies of Cricket Hill are apparently related to those grown in the gardens of China some 1,300 years ago. The Furmans continue to follow traditional planting methods still used in China today, as they expand their cultivated areas. A visit to this unusually inviting nursery is an enriching experience: Aside from enjoying the beauty and peace of the site, you can learn a great deal. You are free to walk around at will, without pressure to buy, although you might well be tempted to try your hand at starting a collection of your own.

✻ **Admission:** Free

Garden open: Wednesday through Sunday 10:00 A.M. to 4:00 P.M. in season.

Further information: Cricket Hill Garden is located in Litchfield County.

Directions: From I–95 or I–84 take Route 8 north to the Thomaston exit (exit 38). Turn left onto Main Street and follow it to Route 254; go left and north for ½ mile to a blinking light. Turn left at Walnut Hill Road and continue up the hill for about 1 mile. Cricket Hill Garden is on the right.

7. Harkness Memorial State Park

275 Great Neck Road, **Waterford**, CT 06385
(860) 443–5725, www.harkness.org

*D*ISCOVERING HARKNESS Memorial State Park for the first time is an unexpected—and joyful—surprise. You are sure to wonder why it hasn't been on your—or everybody else's—itinerary for all these years. This magnificent public park, on the Connecticut shore overlooking Long Island Sound, may well be one of the better-kept secrets in the region.

The combination of spectacular ocean views, sweeping lawns extending to the sea, fine formal gardens surrounding a romantic Italianate mansion, magnificent old trees, and vast areas for walking along the beach, across fields, and on shaded paths, makes Harkness Park unusually inviting. You can easily see why this site might inspire painters. (In fact, on our last visit we saw some local artists at work, trying to capture the scene.) The contrasting shapes and colors are a feast to the eye—from the intimate garden rooms set off by broad sky, land, and sea, to the brilliantly colored flowers, graceful statuary, topiary shapes, and meandering pathways.

The 234-acre estate (100 acres of which have since been developed into a camp for handicapped children) was one of the summer homes of philanthropists Edward and Mary Harkness. Situated on Goshen Point, a promontory where the Pequot Indians once camped, it was named Eolia, after the mythical wind god. (You'll find the site quite breezy, but pleasantly so.) The elegant—but unpretentious—limestone mansion was built in 1902, its forty-two rooms, terraces, and porticoes affording lovely panoramic views.

In 1919 the Harkness family hired the well-known landscape designer Beatrix Jones Farrand to refurbish some of the existing gardens surrounding the house. Farrand designed the plantings for the Oriental east garden to complement its stone wall, statues, and pool; she created a picturesque rock garden, with a stone path bordered by beds of wildflowers; and she revamped the Italian west garden. In the latter, using an existing limestone pergola as centerpiece, Farrand planted her trademark perennials grouped by color, from the softest of blues and mauves to intense shades of orange and yellow.

In subsequent years, other landscape designers were called upon to add their artistic touch to the gardens. Marian Coffin, who had worked on so many of Long Island's sumptuous estates as well as on Winterthur in Delaware, favored a pastel color scheme. She planted flower beds in delicate pinks, lavenders, and whites. The gardens you see today—some of which are yet again undergoing restoration—are an appealing blend of several design styles. Upon Mrs. Harkness's death in 1950, the property was bequeathed to the state of Connecticut to be turned into a public park.

Today's visitor will find Harkness Park a true respite from the bustling outside world. Rarely crowded, it is a treat for garden lovers and walkers of all ages—including children. There is a feeling of informality about the place; you can walk at will from one end of the park to the other, unhampered by the many restrictions found in most public sites. The mile-long beach is easily accessible by foot and a year-round pleasure for anyone, including families. Even off-season it is an ideal spot for kite flying, picnicking, fishing, or just walking.

The gardens are to be savored at a leisurely pace. Contained within a small area around the mansion, they face the ocean. On one side of the house is the Oriental garden, with fountains, statues, and patterned flower beds. An open porch on the other side overlooks the romantic Italian garden. Surrounded by trimmed boxwood hedges, it contains colorful flower beds and the previously mentioned raised pergola, now covered with grape and wisteria vines. Small pathways lead to the rockery, intriguing with its sunken paths, small patterned plantings, and secluded grotto. Beyond are cutting gardens near a water tower, greenhouses, stables, and extensive lawns.

> ❀ **Admission:** Small parking fee in summer.
> **Garden open:** Daily 8:00 A.M. to sunset.
> **Further information:** Harkness Memorial State Park is on Route 213. During the summer occasional classical music and jazz concerts are held under a tent on the main lawn.
> **Directions:** From the New York area: Take I–95 to exit 74, then take Route 161 to its end. Make a left onto Route 156 to Route 213 and follow the signs to the park.

8. Private Garden of Susan and Robert Beeby

Westport, CT, (203) 255-6463

*I*T IS ALWAYS a pleasure to visit a private garden: By definition, you know it won't be crowded or commercial. Susan and Robert Beeby's garden on Connecticut's coastline is not only unspoiled, as you would expect, it is also a beautifully designed garden, combining both new and re-created plantings. A walk along its inviting paths leads from one enchanting spot to the next—from Giverny-like water-lily ponds, graceful waterfalls, and Japanese-style rock formations, to banks of wildflowers, trellises adorned with blossoms, and old-fashioned flower beds.

The story of how this garden came to be is intriguing. On this site there once existed the so-called Bedford Gardens, created in 1912 by local philanthropist Edward T. Bedford. A true lover of nature, Bedford was apparently happy to share his gardens with the public, even though they were on his private estate. Until the late 1930s they were a popular destination, attracting thousands of visitors. Unfortunately, Bedford's heirs were unable to keep the gardens open, and they eventually sold the estate.

When the Beebys bought the property in 1980, there was no sign of the historic gardens. Their many intricate stone structures— pathways, walls, stairways, fountains, decorative pools, and terraces—and vast, sloping lawns were all buried under piles of weeds and unkempt vines. Even Bedford's mansion and greenhouses had been destroyed.

With tireless diligence, the Beebys cleared the land and—like archaeologists—uncovered the lost gardens. Much of the original maze of waterways, stone structures, and greenery has been restored. What had once been banks of rhododendron, andromeda, and boxwood were resurrected; masses of wild daylilies were replanted where they were found to have graced the base of a slope; and the former elaborate water channels, pools, and waterfalls were refurbished and integrated with new plantings. (The original stone piping system is now used only as a decorative feature.)

The gardens extend from the owners' Provence-style house and terrace, one smoothly flowing into the next, up and down the gently sloped terrain. With the help of landscape architect James Bleuer, the Beebys have devised new planting schemes to which they have added artifacts and sculptures collected on their world travels over the years. Among these decorative and artistic touches are a pair of elegant cranes from Thailand standing tall on the edges of both pools, surrounded by masses of flowering shrubbery and rocks.

❀ **Admission:** Free.

Garden open: By appointment only.

Further information: To visit the Beeby's private garden, located in the Green Farms section of Westport, you must phone them first. They will give you the necessary directions.

Don't Miss . . .

9. Larsen Sanctuary of Connecticut Audubon Society

2325 Burr Street, **Fairfield**, CT, (203) 259–6305

www.ctaudubon.org/centers/fairfield/fairfield.htm

THIS SITE WILL not only appeal to bird watchers but also to those interested in horticulture. You'll find a wide variety of native shrubs and herbaceous plants, as well as a trail specially designed for the blind, with a fine collection of fragrant plants.

❀ **Admission:** Fee.

Garden open: Tuesday through Saturday 10:00 A.M. to 5:00 P.M., Sunday noon to 5:00 P.M.

10. Ogden House and Gardens

1520 Bronson Road, **Fairfield**, CT, (203) 259–1598

THE GARDENS connected to this carefully restored (and visitable) 1750 saltbox are of particular interest to both historic garden enthusiasts and lovers of wildflowers. There is an eighteenth-century kitchen garden adjoining the house, as well as an unusually nice native wildflower woodland garden overlooking the river below.

❉ **Admission:** Fee.

   Garden open: Sunday 1:00 to 4:00 P.M. from June through September.

11. Fairchild Connecticut Wildflower Gardens

North Porchuck Road, **Greenwich,** CT, (203) 869–5272

THIS 127-ACRE SITE, part of Greenwich's fine Audubon Center, has 8 miles of trails featuring some ninety-nine varieties of plants. We recommend visiting in spring or early summer for best viewing of the naturalistic landscape (first laid out in the early 1900s by Benjamin Fairchild) and the amazing varieties of wildflowers.

❉ **Admission:** Free.

   Garden open: Daily 9:00 A.M. to 5:00 P.M. from February to September; Thursday through Sunday 9:00 A.M. to 5:00 P.M. from October to January.

12. Nook Farm

351 Farmington Avenue, **Hartford,** CT 06105
(860) 522–9258 and 247–0998
www.harrietbeecherstowecenter.org and www.marktwainhouse.org

THIS HISTORIC COMPLEX includes the adjoining houses and gardens of Harriet Beecher Stowe and Mark Twain. The Stowe garden was restored from old photographs, and, like its neighbor, is intimate and Victorian in style. You can tour both houses for memorabilia and historical anecdotes.

❉ **Admission:** Fee.

   Garden open: Daily 10:00 A.M. to 4:00 P.M. from June 1 to September 1.

13. Sundial Herb Gardens

Brault Hill Road, **Higganum,** CT, (860) 453–2186
www.sundialgardens.com

ALONG A WINDING ROAD lined with stone walls and fine old shade
trees typical of rural Connecticut, you'll see a pretty courtyard with
weathered fences and potted trees next to a charming old barn.
Behind are the Sundial Herb Gardens, a rich collection of diverse
herbs and topiary plants. Any herb enthusiast won't want to miss
this spot. Guided tours are conducted through the well-maintained
and tidy gardens.

Before or after your visit you can enjoy an English-style tea elegantly served in an intimate tearoom, where you can sample dishes
made with some of the herbs grown on the property. Reservations
are necessary.

❀ **Admission:** Fee.

Garden open: Friday, Saturday, and Sunday 10:00 A.M. to 5:00 P.M. in
July, August, and September.

14. Topsmead State Forest

Route 118, 2 miles west of Route 8, **Litchfield,** CT

THIS 40-ACRE wildflower preserve and nature trail is in a 514-acre
forest donated to the state by Edith Morton Chase.

❀ **Admission:** Fee in season.

Garden open: Year-round.

15. White Flower Farm

Route 63 (just south of Litchfield), **Morris,** CT
(860) 567–8789, (800) 503–9624, www.whiteflowerfarm.com

THOUGH PRIMARILY a large, commercial nursery, this beautiful
spot also features open meadows, stone walls, many flower beds (all

plants with identification tags), and fine views. Among the pleasures here: a dwarf evergreen collection that comes from cuttings from the National Arboretum, a greenhouse of tuberous begonias, and a rose garden filled with labeled varieties.

✿ **Admission:** Free.
  Garden open: Daily from April to October, and weekends in winter.

16. Olive W. Lee Memorial Garden

89 Chichester Road, **New Canaan,** CT, (203) 966–6306

THIS SMALLISH BUT unusually pretty woodland garden is planted with daffodils, ferns, laurels, and rhododendrons on hilly terrain with winding paths. Especially nice in spring.

✿ **Admission:** Free.
  Garden open: Seasonally.

17. Edgerton Park

Whitney Avenue and Cliff Street, **New Haven,** CT
(203) 777–1886

THIS IS A most unusual park; originally designed as an English landscape garden to emphasize the importance of open space, it is now on the National Register of Historic Places. In addition to enjoying the landscape itself, visit the Crosby Conservatory, which offers a simulated rain forest and tropical plantings, as well as all kinds of horticultural exhibits.

✿ **Admission:** Free.
  Garden open: Year-round.

18. Connecticut College Arboretum

Williams Street, **New London,** CT 06320, (860) 439–5020

THIS WONDERFUL ARBORETUM and the Native Plant Collection occupy several areas of the college campus. (Pick up a self-guiding tour brochure at the entrance at Williams Street.) You'll find more than three hundred varieties of native trees and shrubs, with ponds and walkways covering some 425 acres. Originally designed for the education of botany students, the arboretum has become a spectacular site; telephone for month-to-month listings of what's in bloom —from mountain laurel to sweet pepperbush.

❀ **Admission:** Free.
Garden open: Daily dawn to dusk.

19. Bartlett Arboretum

University of Connecticut, 151 Brookdale Road, **Stamford,** CT (203) 322–6971

EACH OF THE many trails within this sixty-three-acre arboretum has a special ecological or botanical orientation: There are woodland and wetland trails, a nut tree walk, and rhododendrons, conifers, and azaleas from around the world. Small bridges and walkways take you through the marshes, and you can walk on a path of pine needles in the Needle Evergreen Walk.

❀ **Admission:** Free.
Garden open: Daily dawn to dusk.

20. Old Fort Stamford

900 Westover Road, **Stamford,** CT, (203) 977–4692

HIDDEN WITHIN rural winding roads high above Stamford is a tiny, eighteenth-century-style enclosed garden at a site called the Old

Fort. The fort itself is gone, but what remains is an idyllic garden with an Italianate balustrade, colorful plantings, and a pretty wisteria trellis. Expanses of lawn surround Old Fort Stamford, adding to its appeal. Children will love this spot.

❀ **Admission:** Free.
   Garden open: Daily.

21. Stamford Museum and Nature Center

39 Scofieldtown Road, **Stamford,** CT, (203) 322–1646

IF YOUR TASTE in gardens runs as much to sculpture as to plantings, visit the nature center here, where (mostly) contemporary sculpture dots the landscape. Follow the woodland trail through a lovely setting surrounding a former mansion to see both art and nature nicely combined.

❀ **Admission:** Fee.
   Garden open: Monday through Friday 9:00 A.M. to 4:00 P.M., Saturday 10:00 A.M. to 5:00 P.M., Sunday 11:00 A.M. to 4:00 P.M.

22. Adam's Garden of Eden

360 North Anguilla Road, **Stonington,** CT
(860) 599–4241

THERE ARE FIVE acres of themed gardens here, as well as a Victorian gazebo, herbs galore, and a variety of decorative seasonal displays. While this is a commercial nursery and flower grower for special events, visitors are welcome to wander around, dig and pick their own mums and pumpkins (among other growing things), and even take hayrides in the fall.

❀ **Admission:** Free.
   Garden open: Year-round.

23. Stonington Vineyards

523 Taugwonk Road, **Stonington,** CT
(860) 535–1222

IF YOU HAVE never walked through a vineyard in late summer or early fall, you are missing an unusual and heady treat. Vineyards are springing to life all over New England, and this one is a particularly nice one to walk through. You can take a guided tour or wander on your own through the fifty-eight acres of fragrant grapes.

❀ **Admission:** Fee for guided tour only.
Garden open: 11:00 A.M. to 5:00 P.M. year-round.

24. Elizabeth Park

Prospect and Asylum Avenues, **West Hartford,** CT
www.elizabethpark.org

IN THIS well-known urban rose garden, you can enjoy thousands of old and new species. Be sure to visit in June, during the peak flowering period.

❀ **Admission:** Free.
Garden open: Daily sunrise to sunset.

25. Gertrude Jekyll Garden at the Glebe House Museum

Hollow Road, **Woodbury,** CT
(203) 263–2855, www.theglebehouse.org

GERTRUDE JEKYLL was a distinguished English garden designer of some four hundred notable sites—almost all of them in Britain. This is the only Gertrude Jekyll garden maintained in the United States. Jekyll is particularly noted for her emphasis on border plantings based on color. The component parts of a Jekyll border—shrubs, annuals, bulbs, perennials, small trees, and even potted plants—were all arranged with an eye toward color patterns. While her "cottage" gardens seemed informal and perhaps accidental, in fact each plant was part of a sophisticated composition in color and architectural design.

Though it is not large, Glebe House's elegant, geometric design and profusion of plantings make it both orderly and lush. Created in 1927 for the opening of the Glebe House Museum (the eighteenth-century house is considered to be the birthplace of the American Episcopal Church), the newly restored site includes a rose allée leading to the rose quadrants, a terrace of flowers, a kitchen herb garden, and—Jekyll's specialty—some 600 feet of mixed herbaceous and perennial border. A chart available at the house identifies each of the ninety varieties of plantings and their locations. The blooms are at their best in summer.

❀ **Admission:** Fee.

Garden open: Wednesday through Sunday 1:00 to 4:00 P.M., from April to November.

Gardenwalks in Maine

lowers have an expression of countenance as much as men or animals. Some seem to smile, some have a sad expression, some are pensive and diffident, others again are plain, honest and upright.

—HENRY WARD BEECHER

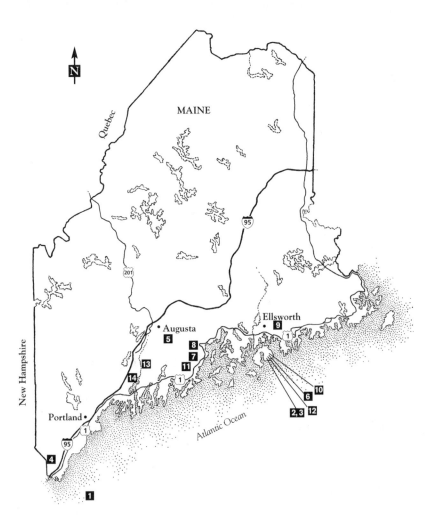

1. Appledore Island: Celia
   Thaxter's Garden
2. Northeast Harbor: Asticou
   Azalea Garden
3. Northeast Harbor: Thuya Lodge
   Garden
4. South Berwick: Hamilton House
   Garden

Don't Miss . . .

5. Augusta: Blaine House
6. Bar Harbor: Wild Gardens of
   Acadia

7. Camden: Amphitheater
8. Camden: Merryspring
9. Ellsworth: Woodlawn, the
   Colonel Black Mansion and
   Gardens
10. Mount Desert: Garland Farm
11. Rockport: Children's Chapel
12. Seal Harbor: Abby Aldrich
    Rockefeller Garden
13. Wiscasset: Nickels-Sortwell
    House
14. Woolwich: Robert P. Tristram
    Coffin Wildflower Reservation

1. Celia Thaxter's Garden

Appledore Island, ME, www.sml.cornell.edu/garden/pg-gi.html

*G*ETTING AWAY to an island retreat is an enduring popular fantasy. Among the enticing islands along Maine's rugged coastline that have appealed to garden, nature—and art—enthusiasts over the years is Appledore. To visit this off-the-beaten-track pleasure is to relive a fascinating period in the American garden and art scene.

The ninety-five-acre island, the largest of the barren and somewhat bleak Isles of Shoals, located some 9 miles off the coast of Portsmouth, New Hampshire, is the site of a beloved Victorian garden that was immortalized in many paintings and writings. One of the first seaside summer resorts on the East Coast during the mid- to late nineteenth century, Appledore has had an intriguing history. How this garden was created, how it inspired an entire generation of American artists, and what became of it, all add to the lore and appeal of the island.

As early as the sixteenth century, European fishermen found the tiny cluster of islands to be rich fishing grounds, and they colonized the islands. A thriving fishing industry, unrivaled in New England, brought wealth to the Isles of Shoals for a brief time. After years of neglect, the islands enjoyed a renaissance when summer tourists rediscovered them in the mid-nineteenth century. They liked the romantic, rugged, moorlike beauty, windswept landscape, and ocean views they found there. Thomas Laighton, a businessman from Portsmouth, opened the Appledore House Resort in 1848 to immediate success. With him came his family, including his remarkably creative and charismatic daughter, Celia.

The reputation of Celia Thaxter (her married name) as a poet of distinction grew. She attracted the attention of many of the literary and artistic lions of her time, who became her friends and later visited in the summers at Appledore. These luminaries—the list reads like a cultural *Who's Who* of late nineteenth-century America—included James Russell Lowell, John Greenleaf Whittier, Nathaniel Hawthorne, Harriet Beecher Stowe, Mark Twain, and the painters William Morris Hunt and Childe Hassam, to name a few. They were drawn to the island's stark, wild beauty, true, but especially to the intellectually and culturally stimulating atmosphere Celia provided, and to the enchanting flower-filled lifestyle they could enjoy at the hotel. They were also charmed by the fabled garden she cultivated on a terrace that sloped from her cottage toward the sea. This splendid 50' x 15' plot of brilliantly colored old-fashioned flowers—poppies, hollyhocks, larkspur, among many other varieties—contrasted sharply with the harsh, stark surroundings of rocks, brush, and sea, a contrast that greatly struck many of these artists.

One artist who was particularly inspired by Celia's garden was the impressionist Childe Hassam, who painted it over and over in its many configurations. He and Celia became fast friends and collaborators. When Celia wrote an account of the joys and frustrations of creating a garden in a physically difficult environment in *An Island Garden*, Hassam illustrated it. He joyously depicted the vitality and sparkle of her garden and other views of the Isles of Shoals in hundreds of oils, watercolors, and pastels over a period of more than thirty years.

Celia Thaxter died in 1894 and, with her, her offshore cultural salon and lovely garden. The hotel and her cottage burned down in 1914, and Appledore was almost forgotten. During World War II, the island housed a submarine observation post (a U.S. Army barracks was placed right on what had been Celia's garden) and, finally, in the 1960s, the Shoals Marine Laboratory, which still exists. In the process of restoring some of the old cottages and building new ones, the laboratory directors had the imagination to reconstruct Celia Thaxter's unique garden, using her book as a guideline.

Today the garden has been restored to include more or less everything Celia grew. It can be enjoyed during the summer months by members of the scientific community as well as day-trippers. While on Appledore you should also visit the Laighton family cemetery, a lonely, windswept spot located near her garden; it is here that Celia was buried. Day visitors may also ask for permission to tour the classrooms and labs of the Shoals Marine Laboratory, and can walk along nature trails to spot gulls, snowy egrets, black-crowned herons, or others of the one hundred or so species seen on the island during migrations.

Getting to Appledore requires some planning and money, but we hope you will feel that being on this special site with its melancholy beauty and connections with the past will be inspiring enough to make it worth the effort.

Visitors to Appledore are first taken to nearby Star Island (also a conference center), where there are additional places of interest to see. Nature lovers can walk along the island's rocky coves and cliffs and hope to spot nesting gulls. Be sure to avoid nesting areas during spring and early summer, however; gulls can be quite ferocious and will dive at those who come too close to their nests.

🌸 **Admission:** Fee.

Garden open: Summer months.

Further information: The ferry for day-trippers (one hundred visitors per trip, maximum) sails out of Portsmouth, New Hampshire, at 11:00 A.M., arriving first at Star Island at about noon; from there you are picked up by the Shoals Marine Laboratory launch for the short trip to Appledore. (To reserve the launch, you must phone ahead at 603–862–2994.) The ferry leaves Star Island at 3:00 P.M. for the trip back to the mainland, so that those going on to Appledore have less than three hours to visit. The cost of the ferry is moderate, but we thought admission to the garden was expensive.

Directions: From Boston to Appledore, take Interstate 95 north to the Portsmouth exit, then follow signs to the ferry.

2. Asticou Azalea Garden

Northeast Harbor (Mount Desert Island), ME
(207) 276-5456 (in season)

*I*T MAY SEEM surprising to find a Japanese-inspired oasis like this one in coastal Maine; it is certainly a treat to visit it. Asticou, which is tucked into a woodsy hillside above the bright cobalt sea below, is an exotic, quiet place complete with raked Zen garden, ponds and trickling water and stepping-stones, and, in early summer—a profusion of blooming azaleas.

Asticou is designed for peaceful contemplation and the enjoyment of native-to-Maine plantings—in an Oriental style. But it is not meant to be precisely a traditional Japanese garden. Instead, the designers have borrowed liberally from that style, using such components as stone, moss, water—and azaleas. Thus you'll find native Maine pines pruned to resemble bonsai, lavender heather familiar to the Maine landscape near a garden with raked white sand, or lichen-covered rocks of granite and mossy mounds that may resemble their Japanese counterparts but also look a bit like the shapes of the islands nearby. It is this odd combination of landscape characteristics of northern New England and Asia that makes Asticou so exotic.

The garden is organized into "rooms," each of which has a different feeling or design. You follow a meandering pale gravel path leading from room to room, occasionally picking your way over stepping-stones or a small stone bridge as you cross a trickling brook or approach the lily pond. Many garden rooms are almost enclosed by profuse greenery, so you come upon these different scenes quite by surprise; winding paths through a garden such as this one date back to medieval Japan. Occasionally you'll see typically Japanese stone statuary nestled among shrubbery.

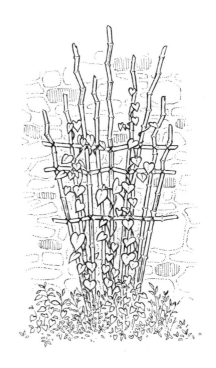

Your route will take you past dozens of different rhododendron and azalea species (best to visit in June when the late spring brings them to their showiest beauty). This is called a "stroll garden," in which your path will lead you by such decorative cultivars as Flame, Pontiac, Snow, Roseshell, and Cumberland azaleas—all of which bloom spectacularly in the salty coastal air here. Flowers and shrubs come from several parts of the Orient (Japanese iris, Chinese flowering cherry, Korean azalea and rhododendron) and from Europe (fothergilla, spring heath, smokebush), as well as from this rocky, mountainous seacoast of Maine.

You will also come to the raked Zen garden, patterned after that of a fifteenth-century temple in Kyoto; here a large area of ashen white sand is perfectly raked into parallel patterns. This is known as a "dry garden"; water and landscape are symbolically represented with raked sand resembling waves and carefully placed rocks suggesting the landscape. (This is the best such dry garden we have seen on our gardenwalks.)

Asticou (which is named for a seventeenth-century Indian chief) was the idea of Charles K. Savage, the same landscape designer who created the gardens at Thuya Lodge nearby. The Asticou area was at that time a swamp of alder thickets and cattails. In

1956, with financial aid from John D. Rockefeller Jr., Savage began to create a fine garden on the property. He constructed two ponds from the swampland, a running stream, and two rolling lawns. He brought a number of azaleas, rhododendrons, and ornamental trees from Reef Point, the coastal Maine gardens of his friend, Beatrix Farrand, the famous horticulturalist. (Reef Point was being dismantled.) With these component parts, granite rocks indigenous to Maine, many additional plantings, and a tranquil Oriental outlook, Asticou gardens were created. Combining both Eastern and Western influences and plantings, they are certainly unique and very lovely. You might wish to combine a visit with Thuya Lodge Gardens just down the road; you will see two very different, very successful approaches to beautiful garden design.

❀ **Admission:** Free.

Garden open: During daylight hours from May 1 through October 31.

Further information: Asticou is located on the northern edge of Northeast Harbor, with the entrance on Route 198.

Directions: Take Routes 3 and 198 to Mount Desert Island. Follow Route 198 to the entrance to Asticou just north of the intersection with Route 3.

3. Thuya Lodge Garden

Northeast Harbor (Mount Desert Island), ME, (207) 276–5133
www.asticou.com/gardens.html

THE PLEASURES of hiking up a beautiful, rocky, pine-covered (but not too steep) mountain directly above a bright cerulean harbor filled with bobbing sailboats is something many of us travel to Maine to enjoy. We relish the sights and delicious ocean air as we climb, and we look forward to the view at the top. Imagine arriving at the summit to discover a giant and oh-so-elegant formal garden as your reward!

Thuya Lodge and its spectacular garden are at the top of Eliot Mountain, a slight mountain, in fact, but high enough to command a wonderful panorama below, and flat enough on top to accommodate a truly magnificent garden. You walk up through the shady woods of spruce and cedar with their alpine plants and lichen-covered boulders on a series of zigzag terraces and handmade stone steps and paths that are never too exhausting, and are surprised with another scenic overlook (and many benches for resting). These walkways are known as Asticou Terraces and are only about a half mile from Asticou Gardens.

The terraces and path up the mountain and the lodge built of white cedar at the top were the creations of Joseph Henry Curtis, a Boston landscape architect who wanted to build his summer residence high above the harbor and deep in the woods. Curtis summered here from 1880 to 1928, and over the years he created on his two hundred acres the amazing system of terraces and the rustic lodge with an orchard behind it. He named the place Thuya Lodge after the *Thuya occidentalis*—or white cedar.

Curtis arranged to transfer the property in perpetuity for the enjoyment of the public. After his death, the trustee of Thuya Lodge (and a landscape designer himself) named Charles K. Savage undertook to turn the big, flat plain of the orchard into a garden and to put the lodge to use as a fine library of botanical books. It was Savage's idea to create a vast formal garden that would be surrounded by—and contrasted with—the natural Maine landscape of granite rock outcroppings, evergreens, and alpine wildflowers.

Savage was fortunate to have financial help from John D. Rockefeller Jr., who summered nearby, and botanical help in the form of plantings from the nearby Reef Point gardens that belonged to Beatrix Farrand, one of America's most notable garden designers. In fact, Farrand's ideas about landscape design are everywhere in evidence at Thuya Lodge Garden, for she devoted much thought to coastal Maine's particular climate and terrain, and Savage was both a friend and disciple. We can see elements of her taste for the formal and geometric tempered by profuse, English-style plantings. Among the especially notable contributions from Farrand's garden are two Alberta spruce that flank the stone steps of the cross axis.

The task of constructing gardens at the top of a mountain apparently did not daunt Mr. Savage and his cohorts. Thuya Gardens are vast, a masterpiece of coherent design. The entrance is a gate through a cedar stockade fence (to keep the deer out); even the gate is artistic: a carved series of designs from a 1629 gardening book—complete with animal symbols and native American plants.

On entering the gate you are taken by a thrill of surprises: A tremendous garden lies before you. A central north–south axis of grass is bordered with double-sided, English, Gertrude Jekyll–style perennial planting beds in bright, appealing colors and varied textures (all labeled); at one end of the axis is an asymmetrical reflecting pool and at the other a special pavilion for contemplation. On either side of these borders are curving paths leading into still other areas of beauty. A cross axis divides the planting beds. Flowers are planted in subtly graduating colors, perhaps making the garden seem even longer than it is.

But a formal description does not begin to capture the ambience of this garden—the areas of quiet shade and brilliant color, the winding paths, and everywhere a delightful use of free-form granite steps and walls and indigenous boulders. And surrounding the cultivated areas is the continued presence of the Maine woods, never very far away. Despite the rigorous design structure, this is a garden that allows natural beauty its full flowering—it feels thoroughly informal!

You can easily spend half a day here exploring the delights of this garden (and perhaps resting up for the downward descent on the many benches and even sofa cushions provided). These gardens are frequently described as the most beautiful gardens in Maine, so allow plenty of time for your visit.

✿ **Admission:** Donation requested.

Garden open: Thuya Lodge Garden is open 7:00 A.M. to 7:00 P.M. July through September; the lodge is open 10:00 A.M. to 4:30 P.M. July 1 to Labor Day.

Further information: The entrance to Asticou Terraces for the climb up to the Thuya Lodge Gardens is on Route 3. Parking is on the right; cross the street at the zebra walk to find a small sign indicating the gardens.

Directions: Take Route 198 onto Mount Desert Island (in the direction of Northeast Harbor) to the intersection with Route 3. Go ⁴⁄₁₀ mile south on Route 3 to the parking area. From Asticou Gardens (if you wish to combine a visit) you can walk out the back gate of Asticou about ⁴⁄₁₀ mile to the entrance.

4. Hamilton House Garden

Vaughan's Lane, **South Berwick,** ME, (207) 384-5269
www.spnea.org/visit/homes/hamilton.html

*W*E SELDOM SEE a formal garden surrounded by the wildest of natural panoramas. But Maine provides that kind of wonderful setting. If you are traveling through southern Maine, this spot is well worth a detour. High on a bluff with a spectacular view of the Piscataqua River and its wetlands and surrounding woods is this stark, white, unadorned 1785 house and its windswept, but curiously formal, garden.

This combination of wilderness and tamed nature in juxtaposition is intriguing. (The owners—the Society for the Preservation of New England Antiquities—must know it; there are three little chairs set at the top of the hill in the garden for contemplation of the panorama.)

The place has an interesting history. It was built by Col. John

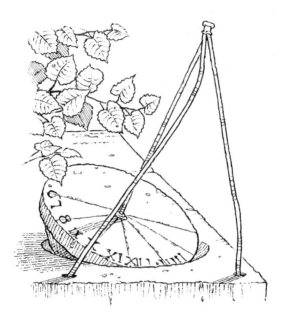

Hamilton, who made his fortune in shipping; but the embargo of
the War of 1812 ruined him, and he sold the three hundred-acre
estate. It was a sheep farm from the 1830s to 1898, when it was sold
once again and fell upon hard times. As a great house in a romantic setting, it intrigued Sarah Orne Jewett, the Maine writer who
visited it as a child and even set one of her novels there. She persuaded Mrs. Emily Tyson to buy it and restore it to its former
grandeur. Mrs. Tyson replanted the gardens in an old-fashioned
style and built a pergola and summerhouse. Her daughter, Mrs.
Henry Vaughan, presented it to the public in 1949.

Created at the turn of the twentieth century by Mrs. Tyson, the
hedged garden is ornamented with terraces and statuary and even
a sundial. There are little pathways and steps here and there and
occasional big round granite grinding wheels to walk on in each terraced level. Plantings include symmetrical beds with boxwood
hedges; many larger bright perennials are charmingly edged with

smaller pastels. The garden has a little gate to a farther shady space. Since you are on top of the hill, there is a view below whichever way you turn.

All of the grounds around Hamilton House, in fact, are beautiful in one way or another. The paths are lined with flowers. And as you walk up to the house and garden from the field below (where you leave your car), there are wildflowers galore (including lots of brilliant purple lupines and tiger lilies) all around you. (You will also find Vaughn Woods Memorial State Park adjacent, for picnicking and hiking). This is a place where your delight in nature—whether untamed or carefully designed—will be gratified, and where you can truly hear the birds sing.

❀ **Admission:** Fee.
Garden open: Hamilton House is open Tuesday, Thursday, Saturday, and Sunday 1:00 to 5:00 P.M. from mid-June to mid-September. (But you can visit the grounds on other days.)
Further information: Tours of the house are offered.
Directions: From I–95 take Route 236 north; after the junction with Route 91, take the first left onto Brattle Street to Vaughan's Lane and follow signs.

Don't Miss . . .

5. Blaine House (State Executive Mansion)

State and Capitol Streets, **Augusta,** ME, (207) 287–2301
www.maine.gov/firstlady/blainehouse/friends.html

BLAINE HOUSE, once the home of James Blaine, a presidential candidate in 1884, has a three-acre garden surrounding it; there are formal plantings and borders of shrubs at this pretty spot.

❀ **Admission:** Fee.
Garden open: Tuesday through Saturday year-round.

6. Wild Gardens of Acadia

Sieur de Monts Spring, Acadia National Park, **Bar Harbor,** ME
(207) 288–3338, www.nps.gov/acad/home.html

IN CONTRAST WITH the formal gardens elsewhere on Mount Desert Island, these are gardens that display plants native to the varied terrain of Maine. Founded in the great Acadia National Park in 1961, these gardens now have some four hundred native species of flowers, ferns, and fruits. There are ten specific areas of plants indigenous to such habitats as bogs, rocky mountainsides, saltwater, meadow, heath, and woodlands.

A small stream fed by the Sieur de Monts spring provides a natural setting for many woodland plants like ostrich ferns, and well-placed granite boulders re-create the rocky habitat for alpine flowers, Bar Harbor juniper, and mountain cranberry. There is even a seaweed-filled beach re-creation to provide a home for saltwater plants like sea lavender and spreading silver and gold potentilla.

The layout is simple; you follow a winding path (which provides occasional stepping-stones), and everything is labeled. For anyone interested in natural plantings and wildlife—of the botanical sort—these are nicely presented and compact gardens, and the wildflower collection is one of the most important in the nation. There is also a museum with educational offerings.

❀ **Admission:** Free.

Garden open: Daily 8:00 A.M. to 8:00 P.M. from May through September.

7. Amphitheater

Atlantic Avenue, **Camden,** ME

BEHIND THE LIBRARY and overlooking the harbor is a fine park: a hillside site with profuse plantings, stone walls, and a fine amphitheater that shows how pretty a public space in the center of a town can be.

❀ **Admission:** Free.
   Garden open: Year-round.

8. Merryspring

End of Conway Road, off Route 1, **Camden,** ME
www.merryspring.org

MERRYSPRING IS A sixty-six-acre site devoted to indigenous Maine flowers, shrubs, and trees. In addition to nature trails and a ten-acre arboretum, there are six acres devoted to flowers: You'll find excellent wildflowers and a woodland garden, as well as cultivated gardens including a lily garden and a rose garden. Great views too.

❀ **Admission:** Free.
   Garden open: Daily dawn to dusk.

9. Woodlawn, the Colonel Black Mansion and Gardens

Route 172 (Surry Road), **Ellsworth,** ME
www.woodlawnmuseum.com/park.html

THIS 1902 Georgian mansion and carriage house on a hill has a very pretty restored formal garden behind it. What distinguishes the flower garden (laid out in 1903) is the lilac hedge surrounding it. Cut to about 4 feet, and uniformly pruned, the lilacs make an unusual and sweet-scented border. Best to visit in June when they are in full bloom, but you'll find the gardens lovely all through the season with perennials and other plantings.

❀ **Admission:** Gardens are free.
   Garden open: House and grounds are open 10:00 A.M. to 5:00 P.M. from June 1 to October 15.

10. Garland Farm

Mount Desert Island, ME 04660
www.members.aol.com/SaveGarlandFarm

THE GREAT AMERICAN garden designer Beatrix Farrand created this exquisite garden, now being renovated. This, her last home and garden, was created in 1955; it features a sea of heather, lilacs, lavender, a little walled garden, cherry trees, and shrub roses all amidst a rocky Maine landscape.

❀ **Admission:** Donation requested.
Garden open: By appointment only. Write to the Beatrix Farrand Society, P.O. Box 111, Mount Desert, ME 04660.

11. Children's Chapel

Vesper Hill, **Rockport,** ME

THIS VERY SIMPLE and touching site high on a hill overlooking the ocean is dedicated to the young. There is a hand-built wooden open-air chapel surrounded by a profuse flower garden and a Biblical herb garden, all of it lovely.

❀ **Admission:** Free.
Garden open: Year-round.

12. Abby Aldrich Rockefeller Garden

Off Route 3, **Seal Harbor,** ME, (207) 276–3330 (in season)

THESE EXQUISITE gardens on a hill above the sea on Mount Desert Island are open to the public only a few times a year by appointment well in advance. Beatrix Farrand collaborated with Mrs. John D. Rockefeller in the 1920s to create this immense garden surrounded by a wall of glazed tiles (from the Imperial Palace in Beijing). Needless to say, you'll find this garden with its Oriental touches midst the

Maine woods and rocks unlike any you've ever seen.

❀ **Admission:** Fee.
Garden open: Thursday from July to September.

13. Nickels-Sortwell House

Corner of Main and Federal Streets, **Wiscasset,** ME
www.spnea.org/visit/homes/nickels.html

IN THE CENTER of this waterside village is a historic house whose
back gardens are now in the process of restoration. But just across
the side street, on the site of an old hotel that burned down in 1903,
is a lovely garden that Frances Sortwell created in 1912. It is an oasis
in the middle of the bustling summer scene.

This deeply sunken garden (its entrance is the short flight of
stone steps down that once led to the hotel's front door) has been
presented to the town and is kept in flourishing condition—filled
with blooming flowers and surrounded by lilacs and shade trees.
There are charming parallel brick paths, a bird bath, a table and
chair for picnicking or contemplation, both bright sun and brilliant
pinks and oranges and purples, and deep shade and darkest greens.

❀ **Admission:** Fee.
Garden open: Visit June through September.

14. Robert P. Tristam Coffin Wildflower Reservation

Merrimeeting Bay, **Woolwich,** ME, www.newfs.org

ONE HUNDRED AND seventy-five acres of tidal marsh, woods, and
fields, much of it home to a great assortment of wildflowers and ferns.

❀ **Admission:** Free.
Garden open: Year-round; visit in summer.

Gardenwalks in Massachusetts

*I*t is not necessarily those lands which are the most fertile
or most favored climate that seem to me the happiest, but
those in which a long stroke of adaptation between man and
his environment has brought out the best qualities of both.

—T. S. ELIOT

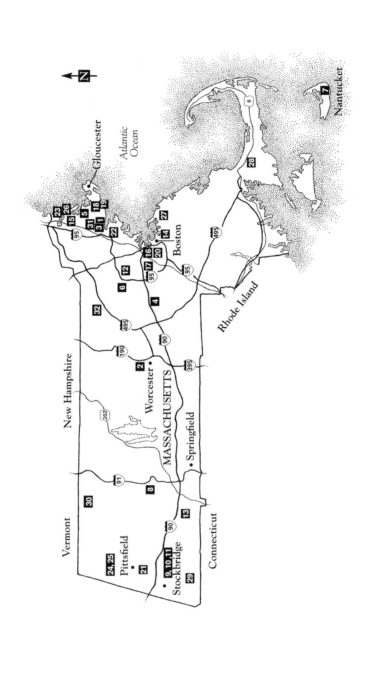

1. Beverly: The Sedgwick Gardens at Long Hill
2. Boylston: Tower Hill Botanic Garden
3. Danvers: Glen Magna
4. Framingham: Garden in the Woods
5. Ipswich: Castle Hill, the Richard T. Crane Jr. Memorial Reservation
6. Lincoln: Codman House
7. Nantucket: Cliff Walk
8. Northampton: Smith College
9. Stockbridge: Berkshire Botanical Garden
10. Stockbridge: Chesterwood
11. Stockbridge: Naumkeag
12. Waltham: The Vale, the Lyman Estate
13. Westfield: Stanley Park

Don't Miss . . .

14. Boston: Isabella Stewart Gardner Museum
15. Byfield: Newbury Perennial Gardens
16. Cambridge: Longfellow House
17. Cambridge: Mount Auburn Cemetery
18. Gloucester: Beauport, the Sleeper McCann House
19. Gloucester: Hammond Cast
20. Jamaica Plain: Arnold Arboretum
21. Lee: October Mountain State Forest
22. Marblehead: Jeremiah Lee Mansion Gardens
23. Newburyport: Maudslay State Park
24. Pittsfield: Hancock Shaker Village
25. Pittsfield: Pleasant Valley Wildlife Sanctuary
26. Plum Island: Parker River National Wildlife Refuge
27. Quincy: Adams National Historic Site
28. Sandwich: Heritage Museums and Gardens
29. Sheffield: Butler Sculpture Park
30. Shelburne Falls: Bridge of Flowers
31. Topsfield: Ipswich River Sanctuary
32. Westford: Butterfly Place

1. The Sedgwick Gardens at Long Hill

572 Essex Street, **Beverly,** MA, (978) 921–1944
www.thetrustees.org/pages/314_long_hill_cfm

*T*HE SEDGWICK GARDENS at Long Hill, on Boston's picturesque North Shore, offer an inviting collection of garden
rooms that wind seamlessly in and out of the surrounding woods.
These shrub and tree gardens, accented by herbaceous plants, cannot be seen all at once: You discover them gradually, as you walk up
and down the hilly site on grassy paths, from one hidden spot to the
next, amid flowering trees, shady groves, and terraced lawns. Children should not miss these "hide and seek" delights.

Combining formal and informal design elements, the gardens
include ornamental features—a circular ironwork pavilion from
France at the edge of a croquet lawn, a Chinese gate from Beijing,
an assortment of graceful statuary—set on lawns that seem, literally,
to be cut out from the woods. Decorative ponds with water lilies and
lotus flowers, and an impressive array of flowering trees (some quite
unusual for this northern climate), are complemented by panoramic
views of the countryside.

The gardens of this 114-acre estate were originally designed by
Mabel Cabot Sedgwick, a horticulturist and enthusiastic writer on
gardens. (She and her husband, Ellery Sedgwick, editor of the
Atlantic Monthly and an author, had purchased the property in 1916
for a summer home.) To existing pasture, wetlands, and woodlands,
she added many plantings: mountain laurel, rhododendron, dramatic
weeping Japanese cherries, lilacs, roses, azaleas, and colorful spring
bulbs. After her death in 1937, the family further embellished the
gardens with a fine collection of tree peonies, Japanese maples, crab

apples, and other flowering examples that today make the gardens brightly colored throughout the growing season. With the collaboration of the Arnold Arboretum in Boston, the plant collection has grown over the years to some four hundred species, all carefully identified and labeled.

The well-tended grounds include a Hosta Garden, Grey Garden, Tree Peony Garden, Cut-flower Garden, South Lotus Pool, and Horseshoe Garden, all surrounding the 1921 house, a replica of the Isaac Ball House in Charleston. Now this stately house contains a comprehensive library featuring books on horticulture and garden design, as well as the offices of the Trustees of Reservations, the owners and managers of the estate since 1957.

You can explore the gardens on your own, or take a guided tour (available by appointment). Long Hill also offers plant sales and a complete horticultural lecture series.

❀ **Admission:** Fee

Garden open: Daily 8:00 A.M. to sunset.

Further information: Sedgwick Gardens are about 30 miles northeast of downtown Boston. The gardens can be quite buggy in summer, so bring insect repellent!

Directions: From Boston take Route 128 to exit 18. Turn left on Route 22 (Essex Street) in the direction of Essex and go for 1 mile, bearing left at the fork. You'll find a brick gatepost and sign indicating the gardens.

2. Tower Hill Botanic Garden

11 French Drive, **Boylston**, MA, (508) 869–6111
www.towerhillbg.org

*T*OWER HILL, one of our newest public gardens, is on the site of what was until recently a dairy farm. And what a view those farmers and cows had! Literally at the crest of a good-size hill, this place has wonderful vistas in all directions—and a truly spectacular one of Wachusett Reservoir and Wachusett Mountain in the distance. We loved standing on the wind-blown terrace of Tower Hill and looking out toward these sites and what seems an otherwise untouched wilderness. In contrast, just behind us was a blooming hilltop garden of great charm and careful design. The site also includes walking trails through 112 acres of field and forest.

The Worcester County Horticultural Society (the third oldest such group in the nation) acquired the property before it could be sold for development. Adjacent to the ca. 1740 farmhouse, they built a reception/education center, terraces, walkways and walls, a trellis, a pergola, nice wooden benches, and a variety of well-planned garden areas. Though the whole complex still has a touch of newness, the landscape has been treated with good taste and a minimum of commercialism. The planners tried hard to maintain what was most distinctive about the site, and it is interesting to see a garden starting the process of becoming mature and venerable.

The major flower gardens lie just beside the old farmhouse. Here in old-fashioned profusion in the Lawn Garden are the perennial beds, a series of circular brick walkways, and an imposing wooden pergola. Because of the newness of the plantings, some of the woody plantings are still in containers. Blooming in the Lawn Garden when we visited were red weigela, peonies, azaleas, rhododendrons, and gorgeous purple iris—all laid out in irregularly shaped beds on the hilltop. The pergola provides a picturesque boundary to the Lawn Garden, as well as framing the view beyond.

A special feature of Tower Hill's design is its Secret Garden. Just beyond the pergola is a lower level, not seen from the garden above. But from the pergola the visitor can look down (or walk down) and enjoy fragrant seasonal flowers.

And farther down the hill is a pretty orchard featuring 119 varieties of apples. The adjacent Wildlife Garden—once a trash dump! —is now being designed to attract birds and bats and, eventually, butterflies. A little structure has already been built so that bird-watchers can enjoy the site without mosquitoes annoying them. Other plans for the future include a physic garden, a fragrance garden, and a shade and woodland garden. Clearly those volunteers who are creating Tower Hill can be kept busy here for years!

A visit to Tower Hill is an opportunity to see a landscape taking shape. Most of our country's public gardens are restorations of one or another historic period; Tower Hill is a present-day creation (though not "contemporary" in artistic terms), and it is good to see a new space preserved in such a pretty way.

✤ **Admission:** Fee.

Garden open: April through December 10:00 A.M. to 5:00 P.M. Tuesday through Sunday and holiday Mondays; January through March 10:00 A.M. to 5:00 P.M. Tuesday through Friday. Closed major holidays.

Further information: An excellent trail map and garden guide can be picked up at the center. Picnics permitted.

Directions: From Interstate 90 (the Massachusetts Turnpike) west of Boston, take Interstate 495 north. At exit 25, take Interstate 290 west. Exit at Route 24 north, which is Church Street. Take Church Street toward Boylston to French Drive (just before the center of Boylston) and turn right.

3. Glen Magna

57 Forest Street, **Danvers**, MA, (978) 774–9165
www.glenmagnafarms.org

*U*NEXPECTED" or "picaresque" might best describe these elegant and romantic gardens on 140 acres north of Boston. Both formal and informal gardens adjoin the stately house called Glen Magna (built by the Peabody-Endicott families starting in 1814 and continuing through many generations). There is a surprise wherever you turn here, for the landscape is like a spread-out collection of garden rooms, each with its own style and personality. With its great lawns and avenues of trees, Glen Magna's landscape has a sense of spaciousness that make the sudden surprises—a statue here, a gate there, a walled garden, a delicate fountain—particularly pleasing.

Glen Magna is a big white mansion at the end of a long, gracious drive (first planted with elms in 1816 and now bordered with pin oaks). Its story and transformation from working farm and hiding place for cargo during the War of 1812, to elegant summer estate of various Endicotts and Peabodys, is dotted with interesting historical tidbits. (Pick up a flyer and guide at the entrance.) We rarely have the opportunity to learn about (and see) how a major garden evolved; perhaps the following thumbnail history will give an idea of why Glen Magna's landscape is so interesting:

In 1814 and 1815, a noted Alsatian gardener named George Huessler laid out the first Peabody gardens around a large tulip tree behind the house on the farm. Then in 1859 the beautiful access road to the farm was made private and Glen Magna became an "estate."

In the 1890s the architectural landscape firm of Olmsted, Olmsted, and Eliot designed the barn road and circular drive in their customary elegance. In 1896 the Italianate garden was set out—in keeping with the fashion for Italian antiquity. Thirty-four years later it was bordered with walls and columns and pergola of imported marble. In 1898 an English-style shrubbery garden was designed by Joseph Chamberlain (father of Neville and an Endicott husband).

In 1901 the most enchanting addition to the landscape was added, when the marvelous eighteenth-century summerhouse was purchased from a nearby farm. Finally, in 1904 the walled rose garden was built behind the summerhouse.

In between, and ever since these major developments, Glen Magna has continued to change. A new garden was being restored when we visited.

This historic overview, however, does not begin to convey the delight of the estate. We walked (with map in hand) through the gardens, marveling at their spaciousness and variety and sheer beauty. We began with the Peabody Gardens, just south of the house. Here peonies (best in June), lilies, hollyhocks, and other perennials bloom in profusion. The 1815 flower-bed design was embellished by Charles Eliot in the 1890s, and it looks just as a New England flower garden should! A gazebo with stone steps leads to Lover's Walk, bordered in arborvitae. The still beauty will transfix you.

The Italianate Perennial Garden is one the high points of the estate. The antique Corinthian marble columns and rustic pergola are absolutely covered with wisteria, and the scent of natural perfumes hangs heavy in the air. A fountain sits in the center of this romantic spot. Against the walls are flower beds filled with high blooms of a great variety of textures and colors.

The shrubbery garden (best in spring) has exotic trees and blooms as well as the more familiar dogwood, azaleas, and forsythia. Its pièce de résistance—and a don't-miss for children as well as adults—is its stupendous weeping beech, so large that you can walk under its great cascading branches into a dark world within and be totally hidden from the green and sunlit outside world.

Nearby is the Derby Summer House (or Tea House), an architectural gem created in 1793. It is now a National Historic Landmark. Built for the Derby farm nearby by a prominent builder and cabinetmaker named Samuel McIntire, this is a confection of design: a two-story federal building complete with delicate columns, festooned window, arched doorways, and two wonderful rooftop statues. (A flyer just about the Summer House is available with the map at the entrance to Glen Magna.) This elegant addition to the gardens overlooks the entire estate and, right below it, the rose garden.

Designed by Herbert Brown in 1904, the garden of roses is ornamented by a marble-topped brick wall and two fountains, one of which has a shallow pool filled with water lilies—a pretty combination with the delicate roses growing around it in a variety of different-size and -shape flower beds.

These are only the high points of a visit; there are also numerous small buildings, columns here and there, Etruscan vases, statues, and walks through the trees.

❁ **Admission:** Donations are accepted for access to the grounds.
 Garden open: Daily 10:00 A.M. to 4:00 P.M. mid-May to mid-October.
 Further information: Glen Magna also has house tours.

Directions: From Route 128 north of Boston, take Route 1 north to Danvers. Take the Center Street exit, turning right off the exit. After less than a mile, you'll see Ingersoll Road and a sign for Glen Magna on your left.

4. Garden in the Woods

180 Hemenway Road, **Framingham**, MA, (508) 877–6574
www.newfs.org/garden.html

*I*F A QUIET WALK in the woods amid wildflowers and native plants sounds appealing, then head for Garden in the Woods, an environmentalist's dream. Located on a choice site of high ridges and deep hollows carved out by glaciers, this natural sanctuary is considered one of the premier wildflower gardens in America. Woodland trails wind through a hilly terrain past ponds and rippling streams, high leafy trees and thick stands of pines, masses of rhododendrons, and vistas of wildflowers, shrubs, and ferns.

This forty-five-acre living museum, owned and operated by the New England Wild Flower Society, contains more than 1,500 varieties of plants, including rare and endangered species. Three miles of well-tended, meandering trails lead to individual gardens specifically designed for each habitat and carefully placed so as to blend with their surroundings. These naturalistic gardens not only feature the woodland, bog, and rock plantings you would expect to find in a woodsy setting, but also, more surprising, meadow and desert varieties. Additional pleasures include a terraced, shaded nursery and natural wooded areas filled with yet more varieties of wildflowers from late April through fall. As you wend your way along the paths, you can feel fresh breezes rustling through the trees (this is a cool spot even on a hot summer day). The underbrush beneath the trees has been cleared selectively, so that you can enjoy views, say from a laurel bend to a ridge of evergreens; and the sun filtering through the trees creates a play of light that adds to the ambience.

Garden in the Woods was developed in the 1930s by Will C. Curtis and Dick Stiles, who were dedicated conservationists. They found this glacier-molded site ideal for creating a garden of wildflowers and rare and diverse species. In 1931 they purchased the thirty-acre tract of land and tirelessly set about clearing paths by hand. Garden in the Woods was formally recognized as a botanical garden in the 1940s; in 1965 it was given to the New England Wild Flower Society, which has operated it to promote conservation of temperate North American plants through education, research, and preservation. (An additional fifteen acres have since been acquired.)

The garden is an active place that offers classes, lectures, workshops, guided tours, plant sales, and exhibits. There is a visitor center, a well-equipped museum shop, and library; but the atmosphere is surprisingly low-key, making it a popular place for families and ideal for children to explore.

Before venturing forth you will want to pick up a map and self-guided tour brochure available at the visitor center. The network of paths begins at the nursery area, where plants being propagated for the garden, as well as for research and sales, are on view. Although there is a choice of routes—all well maintained—the main one to take is the Curtis Trail, which leads to the specialized gardens. (You will note that all plants are labeled and that handcrafted wood benches are to be found here and there, for a rest or moment of reflection.)

The first group of gardens on this main itinerary includes a woodland garden, which then opens on to a sunny lily pond and rock garden. The contrast of shaded, canopied vegetation followed by a nice feeling of openness is most inviting.

The next series of gardens—consisting of simulated habitats and including only North American plants—features a laurel bend, tufa rock garden, acid soil rock garden, sunny bog, pitcher plants, pine barrens, western garden, and meadow garden. You might be surprised to discover cactus (in the western garden), or the endangered plants of the New Jersey pine barrens, thriving on necessarily sandy soil. The tufa rock garden, recognizable for its porous rock and alpine plants, contains an unusually high number of rare species; and the meadow garden is a special delight from early summer through fall, when native grasses and brightly colored wildflowers are at their peak. There is a great variety of habitats—perhaps more than you would expect—and you will be tempted to linger at each site, absorbing it all.

The woodland areas come next, with trails looping through so-called second-growth forest (found in middle and southern New England). Many wildflowers also grow here—depending on the season—such as Virginia bluebells, wood phlox, bloodroot, and trout lilies. In late spring the graceful pink lady slippers make their appearance on the hillside of a trail named after them. Along the Hop Brook Trail are ferns, skunk cabbage, and other water-loving plants. With its gurgling book, this is always a refreshing spot. The last of these woodland trails—Lost Pond Trail—runs through hilly terrain and, when it is fully developed, will display rare or endangered plants of New England.

As you make your way back to the parking lot—perhaps disregarding the occasional slightly cutsey signs that congratulate you on having completed this hilly walk, for example—you will no doubt feel you have been on a most unusual and special garden walk.

❀ **Admission:** Fee.

    Garden open: 9:00 A.M. to 5:00 P.M. Tuesday through Sunday from April 15 through October 31.

    Further information: Informal guided walks are conducted on Tuesday through Saturday mornings at 10:00 for individuals; group tours by reservation.

Directions: From Boston or points north or south: Take Route 128 to Route 20. After 8 miles take Raymond Road (the second left after the traffic light in South Sudbury) and go 1.3 miles to Hemenway Road, following signs for the garden.

From points west: Take exit 12 off I–90 (the Massachusetts Turnpike) to Route 9 east. Go 2.4 miles to the Edgell Road exit. At the top of the exit ramp, turn onto Edgell Road and go 2.1 miles to the traffic lights. Take a right onto Water Street, then take your first left onto Hemenway Road.

5. Castle Hill, the Richard T. Crane Jr. Memorial Reservation

Argilla Road, **Ipswich,** MA, (978) 356–4351
www.thetrustees.org/pages/287_castle_hill.cfm

*H*ERE AT CASTLE HILL high above the ocean on the coastal North Shore, with spectacular views in every direction, you will find one of those surprising landscapes of eccentricities created by Americans with a taste for grandeur. Original, idiosyncratic estates like this one make garden visiting intriguing; this landscape was apparently created with sheer bravado—as well as a definite taste for European magnificence of the past. We have not seen anything like these alterations to the natural landscape anywhere in our American garden visits.

We are hardly accustomed to "Roman ruins" in Ipswich, Massachusetts, nor even to the vast elegance of the grand European landscape design found here overlooking the untamed salt marshes, tidal marshes, and sand dunes. But this very unlikely juxtaposition of wild natural beauty with manicured elegance makes a visit here special. (However, if you are only interested in flowers, skip this one . . . there aren't very many.)

First—the views: The surroundings include a 4-mile-long barrier beach and tidal estuaries that are in themselves very beautiful.

Inlets and serpentine rivulets run through the marshy wetlands, sun gleaming—a veritable delight for the landscape artist (and over the centuries many of them have come to paint these Essex and Ipswich River estuaries). The vistas are breathtaking and can be enjoyed from many different vantage points around the mansion that sits at the top of Castle Hill.

As to the estate itself, it was part of a massive parcel of land, including an island, purchased in 1909 by a Chicago industrialist named Richard T. Crane Jr. The original Italianate villa he had built was unsatisfactory and was replaced in 1925 by today's large, brick, Stuart-style fifty-nine-room mansion designed by David Adler; it is open for tours. (Some 1,400 acres of the land surrounding the house have been bequeathed to the Trustees of Reservations and the remaining 165 acres are part of the estate. The reservation is open for hiking and bird-watching, and there is swimming at Crane Beach below.)

Crane had a taste for historical landscape, ranging from Roman to eighteenth-century English. Unfortunately, most of the garden areas have not been restored and, as noted earlier, there are hardly any flowers. Not far from the house are the remains of formal Italian gardens (minus the flowers) designed by the architectural firm of Olmsted. And across the way you'll find what was once a formal circular rose garden, designed by Arthur Shurcliff in 1913–14; appearing today somewhat like a Roman amphitheater and pavilion, its columns are decaying and overgrown with vines. In fact, Crane himself couldn't have asked for a more ancient, ruined-looking setting than what now prevails in these evocative, very romantic, unkempt gardens.

But the most eye-catching sight here is surely the full half-mile mall-like Grand Allée: a very wide, rolling lawn downhill, which has been landscaped to resemble an undulating, unfurling ribbon to the sea. Also designed by Shurcliff, it is a direct translation of the design for the Cypress Allée at the Boboli Gardens in Florence.

There are walking paths among the bordering spruce and English statuary. What a dramatic coastal design this is!

✿ **Admission:** Fee for tours.

Garden open: The house is open for tours on Wednesday and Thursday 10:00 A.M. to 4:00 P.M. from May 1 through October 31, but the grounds and the reservation are open daily year-round.

Directions: Ipswich is north of Boston. Take Route 1A north (exit 20A) from Route 128. Follow Route 1A 8 miles to Ipswich. Turn right onto Route 133 east. Go 1.5 miles to Northgate Road and go left on Northgate .5 mile to Argilla Road. Go right on Argilla Road 2.3 miles to the gate.

6. Codman House

Codman Road, **Lincoln,** MA, (781) 259–8843

www.spnea.org/visit/homes/codman.html

𝒞ODMAN HOUSE combines the charms of a rustic country estate with elegance and style. Located in rural Lincoln, near Boston, the handsome mansion and sixteen acres of rolling terrain provide an inviting setting for a quiet walk. As you stroll through this genteel world of flower gardens, venerable stone walls, and captivating vistas, you could easily imagine yourself a country squire of another era, looking over the land.

The historic house sits gracefully atop a knoll overlooking a broad landscape of meadows and hills. In the mid-eighteenth century, when it was originally built, it was a much simpler structure. John Codman, who bought it in the 1790s, embellished and remodeled it extensively, converting it into a federal-style mansion. The house underwent further transformations during the nineteenth century; today, it is an elegant, symmetrical building combining Georgian, federal, Victorian, and colonial revival architectural styles. A showplace of eighteenth- and nineteenth-century furniture and decorative arts, it can be visited by guided tour.

The grounds are an appealing combination of elegance and informality and can be enjoyed freely; there are no fences or gates surrounding the property. Vast fields, complete with horses, form an idyllic background to the plantings and grassy ha-ha in front. Magnificent rhododendrons and specimen trees, including a rare magnolia and tall horse chestnuts, surround

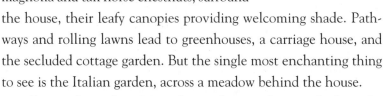

the house, their leafy canopies providing welcoming shade. Pathways and rolling lawns lead to greenhouses, a carriage house, and the secluded cottage garden. But the single most enchanting thing to see is the Italian garden, across a meadow behind the house.

Dating from the 1860s, this sunken garden was laid out by Ogden Codman Jr., designer of some of the grand estates in Newport. (He also was known to have collaborated with Edith Wharton in some of her interior designs.) A charming trellis made of stone columns supports a thick arbor with great clumps of grapes; a lily pond with Italianate statuary is surrounded with urns filled with masses of flowers; and beyond the garden are deep woods, silent except for the sounds of birds. This is, indeed, a peaceful oasis to be savored.

❀ **Admission:** Fee for house; gardens are free.

Garden open: Year-round.

Further information: Codman House is located in Lincoln, about 20 miles west of Boston. The house is open Wednesday through Sunday from June to October 15, and can be seen only by guided tour.

Directions: From Boston: Take Route 2 west to Route 126 (Concord Road) south. Take a left at Codman Road and look for a small sign to Codman House.

7. Cliff Walk

Siasconset Village, **Nantucket,** MA

ANTUCKET IS an alluring island. Some 30 miles out at sea, it offers long stretches of unspoiled beaches and rugged coastline, softly colored moors, picturesque villages, and the intriguing legacy of a once-thriving whaling industry. As inviting are its many private gardens—mostly English-style gardens surrounding seaside villas and guesthouses—and its weathered shingled cottages often literally dripping with climbing roses. In fact, all kinds of flowers seem to proliferate in this surprisingly temperate climate.

You can visit a number of Nantucket's intimate gardens by taking a garden tour, held annually during the summer. Or you can view them while biking or walking along any number of cobblestone streets, country lanes, and rustic paths. One of our favorite of these walks is the so-called Cliff Walk, which combines spectacular ocean panaramas with a row of individual gardens.

Its name notwithstanding, this walk is not physically daunting or demanding; rather, it is a flat, pleasant stroll along masses of wild rose shrubs and grassy walkways. At all times you can enjoy dramatic views of the ocean on one side of the path, and charming garden settings on the other. The walk itself takes about an hour, and you can shorten or lengthen it as you wish.

You start in the village of Siasconset (pronounced simply "Sconset"), behind the Wade Cottages, where a decidedly unobtrusive grassy path "heralds" the walk. (See below for more detailed directions.) The path actually crosses private lawns and gardens attached to their respective houses. (Don't be concerned about invading anyone's privacy, as you are on a public right-of-way.) The path wends its way from one property to the next, alongside old-fashioned flower beds with many colorful varieties, among them hydrangeas, lilies, and roses (which seem to be ubiquitous). Some gardens are enhanced by elegant private hedges surrounding them or forming arched passageways leading to the next property. You will find considerable variety in plantings and garden design; fortunately, however, everything blends in nicely within a basic Nantucket style. On the ocean side of most properties are long expanses of wooden steps connecting the gardens with the sea. They twist and turn somewhat precariously over the cliffs, adding a certain drama to the scene.

Eventually you come to a small sign indicating the end of Cliff Walk. From here you can retrace your steps or, for a different view, circle back on one of the little streets on the other side of the path.

❀ **Admission:** Free.

Garden open: Year-round.

Further information: The best time to take this walk is during the summer months, when most flowers—especially the many varieties of roses, both cultivated and wild—are at their peak. However, the site is equally inviting in early fall, when you are likely to have it mostly to yourself.

Directions: In the village of Siasconset find Main Street. Go past the little sea captains' cottages and turn left onto any of the side streets, which will lead you to Sankaty Road. From there, make your way to Wade Cottages, walk on the right-hand side of the main house to the back, and turn left (east). Here you will find a small path (sometimes difficult to identify because it blends in so well with its surroundings). You have reached Cliff Walk.

8. Smith College

College Lane, **Northampton,** MA, (413) 584–2700
www.smith.edu

*F*EW COLLEGE CAMPUSES take their gardens and botanical laboratories as seriously as Smith College. We recommend a stroll through this wonderfully inviting campus and its conservatories— as both students and visitors have been doing for more than one hundred years. In fact, from its founding Smith has been known for its spacious campus replete with greenhouse with tropical plants, outdoor gardens of all kinds, and intensive botanical courses.

In 1872, in its first handbook, the college listed botany and other physical sciences to which "particular attention will be paid." According to the college, serious study of botanical sciences began almost at once, a landscape firm and botanists were hired, and a building erected for the study of botany. "It is the first time in the history of the world," said the president in 1885, "that a building like this has been devoted to the study of science in a female college."

In the 1890s the landscape firm of Frederick Law Olmsted (of Central Park fame) laid out the huge campus, with instruction to make all of it serve as a botanical garden. Each building was to be surrounded with particular species of trees and plants. The first greenhouse was added in 1894, followed soon after by more green-houses, laboratories, a "succulent house," a palm house, and potting sheds. Smith College obviously intended its campus to be both beautiful and educational.

In 1894 a collection of exotic plants was begun—including dogwoods from China, weeping cherry trees from Japan, maples from Manchuria, and numerous other Asian specialties. More recent renovations have included updated conservatories and ever more trees and plantings as the campus expanded. Despite a harsh New England climate, the college has continually replanted and added to its tree collection. Its greenhouses have been put to exten-sive use, with cool and warm climates, a fern house, and areas for bedding flowers later to be planted throughout the campus.

In fact, a visit to this site may be happily scheduled during one of the two annual flower shows that feature the changing seasons. In spring, dozens of varieties of bulbs are featured—tulips, hyacinths, narcissi, crocuses, and other bulbs set with primroses and azaleas.

These more common American flowers are interspersed with exotic flowers from around the world. In fall, chrysanthemums—both familiar species and rare ones from China—are the centerpiece. Each festival lasts for a week, during which the campus welcomes thousands of visitors.

Your tour of the gardens should include the Lyman Plant House (the major botanical laboratory site), the Rock Garden Area (which includes exotic trees from Asia and a "Ben Franklin tree"), the Herbaceous Garden Area (where you'll find more than forty different species depending on the season, including everything from spiderwort to amaryllis, and cabbages to geraniums and sunflowers), and the Arboretum (with some one hundred types of trees).

If you wish to see the delights of this campus in an orderly fashion, you should begin your walk at the Lyman Plant House and its entry at the Head House. (You will find it is open every day of the year, and you may pick up a campus map there.) The staff even welcomes your questions.

Your tour of the facilities will take you to the Warm Temperate House (don't miss the grapefruit-size lemons and the pale violet water hyacinths). Next, the Stove House features goldfish swimming among such unexpected plants as rice, papyrus, and sugarcane. The Cold House comes next; it is filled with potted plants waiting for the spring, such as primroses and azaleas. Show House (between the Head House and the Cold Storage House) is where the flower shows are held. Beyond the Cold Storage House is a corridor of changing displays and camellias.

Beyond a series of laboratories you'll find the Temperate House, divided into four temperate geographic regions: Asia, Australia and New Zealand, Africa, and the Americas. Here your interest in exotic flora will be satisfied; specimens range from eucalyptus from New Zealand to American avocados.

From here you'll descend a ramp to the Palm House, a veritable jungle of rare palms and lush tropical plants, banyans and bamboo, cacao and cinchona. The Fern House—one of the oldest greenhouses on campus—is next; it too features plants from Asia as well as New England, including specimens from the East Indies and Tasmania. The Cold Temperate House will be next; you'll recognize it by the fragrant flowering olive tree.

On the south side of the Plant House is the Succulent House, specializing in Old World desert plants on your left, and New World deserts to your right. (The origins of these plants reads like an atlas index! Madagascar, Peru, the Sahara . . .)

Beyond these buildings you'll find the outdoor Rock Garden, where, in season, you'll discover an exhaustively wide collection of dozens of plants of international origin—Swiss edelweiss, African violets from the Pyrenees—we could go on and on. Here too is the famous Ben Franklin tree, now almost extinct except in cultivated gardens. The herbaceous garden that you'll come to next is a kind of outdoor laboratory that traces the evolutionary history of flowering plants. There is a pond here too—needless to say, it contains a large assortment of water plants.

You may now continue your walk across the campus to spot the many trees (all identified) and the beautiful layout of Olmsted's design. (We have not mentioned here the many artworks dotting the campus, but they are an added attraction to this outing. Information about them may be found at the college's art museum—also well worth a visit.)

There is a winding path—in springtime bordered by blooming trees and shrubs—and numerous trails that will take you to wonderful regions of mountain laurel in season, a giant redwood tree, and many other lovely places. In fact, you may find a stroll through these wilder regions of the campus your favorite part of the outing. But whatever your taste—for identifying the exotic, or merely for soaking up the perfumed and visual pleasures of the natural world—

you'll find it here. But do be sure to pick up a map to take with you before you set out!

⚜ **Admission:** Free.

Garden open: The campus of Smith College is open at all times to visitors.

Further information: The campus buildings are all wheelchair accessible. The campus itself has a somewhat hilly, rolling terrain that is pleasant for walking but may be difficult for a wheelchair in some places.

Directions: From New York, take the Hutchinson River Parkway to Route 15 (the Merritt Parkway) to the Wilbur Cross Parkway (also Route 15) to Interstate 91 north. Exit at Northhampton and follow signs to Smith College.

9. Berkshire Botanical Garden

Routes 102 and 183, **Stockbridge**, MA, (413) 298-3926
www.berkshirebotanical.org

*W*HILE MANY of our best gardens are restorations of grand estate landscapes of the past, here we have something entirely different and every bit as successful. For the Berkshire Botanical Garden is a homemade—and enchanting—setting that is designed, maintained, and enjoyed by local garden enthusiasts. Its ambience is free and easy, picturesque, unstructured—just the place to spend a Sunday afternoon. And instead of walking sedately through formal garden paths, here you will be tempted to frolic on the great lawn, poke a stick in the woodsy water-lily pond, lean down to smell the tangy aromas in the hillside herb garden, or wander around the profuse flower gardens (many of which are planted around and atop the great glacial rocks that are strewn across the landscape).

We found this setting idyllic on a hot summer day. Among the twenty-three separate planting sites are great trees and brilliant orange, yellow, and pink poppies; rock gardens filled with dianthus and phlox; a rose garden; two greenhouses (one solar); and an herbacious perennial garden. There are also a primrose garden (a lovely idea), an ornamental organic vegetable garden, and two hundred types of daylilies. Everything blooms profusely in season, despite the harsh winters and high winds of western Massachusetts's climate. Part of this garden's charm is its rather ad hoc layout—on two sides of a fairly busy roadway. But the main portion is a grandly sweeping hillside. And no one tells the visitor where to walk or how to enjoy these gardens. (This is one of the best of all our sites to take small children.)

The Botanical Garden (a new name—for years it was the Berkshire Garden Center) was founded by a few like-minded citizens of the Berkshires in 1934. It was designed to be—and still is—an educational center, with numerous programs for children and adults, events, volunteer opportunities, flower shows, and group activities—such as how to create herb vinegar. It remains the only garden center of its kind in a large area.

There is a calendar of blooms, as well as a map identifying the location of each (labeled) plant. The gardens are still very much in process, with new areas being added and cultivated all the time. (No doubt if you live in the region, your horticultural help would be appreciated!) If abundant bright-colored blooms informally set amid a green Berkshire landscape of giant rocks and venerable trees take your fancy, be sure to visit here.

❀ **Admission:** Fee.

Garden open: Daily from 10:00 A.M. to 5:00 P.M. from May through October.

Further information: There are many programs open to the public.

Directions: Stockbridge is reached from I–90 (the Massachusetts Turnpike) by exiting at Lee (if coming from the east) or at West Stockbridge (from the west). From Lee take Route 102 west through Stockbridge to the intersection with Route 183. From West Stockbridge take Route 102 east. From Route 7 at Great Barrington, go to Stockbridge and turn left on Route 102.

10. Chesterwood

Williamsville Road, **Stockbridge,** MA, (413) 298–3579

www.chesterwood.org

*T*HE LOVELY REGION of western Massachusetts known as the Berkshires is endowed with charming vistas, mountains, rivers, lakes, and little New England villages. The area has long attracted seekers of unspoiled natural beauty, including many artists and writers.

Daniel Chester French, the famed neoclassical sculptor of monumental works, came to establish a summer home, studio, and gardens in the shadow of Monument Mountain near Stockbridge, Massachusetts. When you visit Chesterwood, his remarkable country estate, you will come away feeling that he could not have chosen a more idyllic spot. He was an artist who really knew how to live.

French became the nation's leading classical sculptor in the early decades of the twentieth century. At the height of his career, internationally known and able to live in grand style, French decided to create a perfect working and living environment for himself and his family in the country (although he continued to maintain a winter studio in New York). He and his wife first saw the rustic farm that was to become Chesterwood while on a horse-drawn carriage trip through the Housatonic River valley in 1896.

Beautifully situated on a rural road, the 150-acre property—now a museum operated by the National Trust for Historic Preservation—would become the Frenches' summer home for the next thirty-three years. It was at Chesterwood—amid the enchantment of romantic gardens, lawns, and woodlands—that French was inspired to create many of his most important works, including the Lincoln Memorial, the *Minute Man* for Concord, Massachusetts, and the *Alma Mater* for Columbia University.

Chesterwood itself became a lifelong project for the sculptor. Carefully he fashioned the estate to provide an ideal ambience for his creative needs, as well as for the many brilliant social gatherings he was fond of hosting for his prominent neighbors and friends. (Edith Wharton came regularly from her nearby estate.) The main house and studio, overlooking majestic Monument Mountain, were designed by his architect friend Henry Bacon; but it was French himself who laid out the gardens and woodland walks.

To him gardens were like sculptures: A basic design had to be drawn up in order for them to work as art. He planned a central courtyard, an Italianate garden with a graceful fountain, and English flower gardens. Beyond the formal areas he arranged a network of paths leading into and through the hemlock forest, where the walker could enjoy peaceful views. He enjoyed creating aesthetic effects that influenced the quality of daily life. For example, he built a berm (an artificial little hill) abutting the road leading to the house; in that way one could not see the wheels of approaching carriages, which would appear to be floating by.

French spent a great deal of time in his gardens, from which he derived much of his inspiration. He regularly studied the effects of light and shadow on sculptures that were destined to be outdoors. He found an ingenious solution to moving these massive works from his studio to the outside. He would put these pieces onto a revolving modeling table set on a short railroad track and roll them out into the sunlight, where he could test them in the natural light. You can still see this unusual contraption when you visit the studio.

French and his wife lived and thrived at Chesterwood with their daughter, Margaret Cresson French, also a sculptor. In 1969 the property was donated to the National Trust and converted into the museum you see today.

When you arrive at Chesterwood, you are struck by the beauty of the site: With spectacular mountain views on all sides, it is little wonder that French and his family wanted to be here. The house and landscaping are tasteful and harmonious in every sense; there is nothing pretentious or ostentatious about this estate. As the artist once remarked, "I live here six months of the year—in heaven. The other six months I live, well, in New York."

To visit the house and studio you must take an organized tour—about forty-five minutes of fairly detailed information (more than you might want to hear), including a great deal about the social life of the French family and mores of the time. However, you are free to roam the gardens and woods at will, and can do so at no cost. After you have purchased your tickets for the house and studio, you will probably be directed to the barn to begin the tour. This rustic building, originally part of the working farm that French purchased, has been remodeled into an exhibition gallery. You can wander about and look at the vintage photographs and works by Margaret Cresson French, Augustus Saint-Gaudens, and others.

Aside from the gardens, the studio visit is by far the most satisfying part of the tour. The beautifully designed 22-foot-high structure provided the perfect airy and spacious working environment. It is kept much as it was during French's time, with material, notebooks, tools, and sketches on view. You'll see plaster-cast models and preliminary sculptures of some of his most important works, notably his seated Lincoln (of which there are several versions) and his graceful Andromeda. You'll also see the massive 30-foot double doors that were constructed to accommodate French's many large works; they were built when French first made his impressive equestrian statue of George Washington, now located in the Place d'Iéna in Paris. In back of the studio is a wide veranda (which he called a "piazza") with wisteria vines and fine views and the rail tracks on which his massive sculptures rolled away. The thirty-room colonial revival house (built in 1900) is nearby. Its gracious rooms, wide hallways, and appealing surroundings are what you would expect from a man of French's refined tastes. Surrounding the house are the charming gardens that French carefully planned and so enjoyed.

Take a stroll in them and beyond, on the pine-laden woodsy paths in the forest.

❊ **Admission:** Fee.

Garden open: Daily 10:00 A.M. to 5:00 P.M. from May through October 31.

Directions: Chesterwood is about 2 miles west of Stockbridge. From Boston take I–90 (the Massachusetts Turnpike) to exit B3 to Route 22; go about 1 mile to Route 102 to Stockbridge. Take Route 102 west to the junction with Route 183. Turn left onto Route 183 and continue 1 mile to a fork in the road. Turn right onto a blacktop road, travel a few yards, and turn left. Continue ½ mile to Chesterwood.

11. Naumkeag

Prospect Hill Road, **Stockbridge**, MA, (413) 298–3239
www.thetrustees.org/naumkeag.cfm

*N*AUMKEAG—the name is Indian for "haven of peace"—is a must for those who have a yen for unusual landscape design in addition to gardens. For here, surrounding a picturesque Victorian manor designed by Stanford White, are fanciful gardens arranged with real panache. Begun in the 1920s, they represent a bold departure from the ornate designs of the time, and today they appear as fresh and original as ever.

Magnificently situated in the Berkshire hills, with vistas over woodlands and mountains, Naumkeag's gardens are full of surprises. Instead of traditional flower beds and borders and paths, the plantings here are set off by a collection of eclectic features—from a painted Chinese pagoda, to brilliantly colored Venetian-like wooden pillars, to serpentine gravel patterns amid rose beds, to the extraordinary Blue Steps, which alone are worth the trip to the site.

The creative force behind Naumkeag's gardens was Fletcher Steele, a master landscape architect who was a prime mover in the new, modern orientation in garden design just then being introduced. According to Steele, landscape architecture was a fine art, like painting or music—in fact, he saw himself as a landscape sculptor more than anything else. Reacting against the still prevalent nineteenth-century Beaux-Arts formalism, he advocated a style that drew its inspirations from the natural landscape as well as from the artistic movement of the time, abstract modernism. Indeed, his gardens at Naumkeag are abstract landscapes created from the reworking of the land.

When Miss Mabel Choate inherited Naumkeag in 1926 from her father, Joseph Hodges Choate (a prominent lawyer and diplomat who had built the house in the 1890s as an idyllic summer retreat), she was impatient to redo its Victorian gardens. (Aside from aesthetic considerations, the original flower gardens required more maintenance than she thought appropriate.) She met the already well-established Steele in 1926, and a fruitful collaboration between them ensued, lasting through the 1950s. (They were an unlikely pair: she, willful and rooted in her New England ways; he, a sophisticated world traveler.)

After carefully studying the site, Steele concluded: "Neither the client nor her Victorian house, neither Bear Mountain nor the hillside itself wanted a so-called naturalistic affair with a path meandering downhill. A range of terraces in the Italian Garden manner was unthinkable. . . . Italian gardens do not fit Victorian wood houses. The only resource was to create an abstract form in the manner of modern sculpture, with swinging curves and slopes which would aim to make their impression directly, without calling on the help of associated ideas, whether in nature or art."

Steele did not completely dismantle the old gardens, for he felt that "the old spirit should be followed. . . . the 'feeling' of Victorian elaboration must be continued." True, he moved mounds of earth in places to repeat the curves of the mountain's skyline and enhance the setting, and he created entirely new schemes, but he also rearranged and worked around existing plantings.

Today you can walk up and down and around these wonderful gardens and grassy lawns on your own, using the walking guide available at the entrance, or go on a guided tour of house and garden. On the south side of the mansion is Steele's first creation, the Afternoon Garden, where Miss Choate would take her tea overlooking the mountains. (It seems she repeatedly took Steele to task about the uncomfortable metal chairs he had placed there, but her complaints fell on deaf ears; he considered the chairs pieces of the sculpture to be admired, rather than used.) Screening this theatrical garden are ropes festooned with clematis and Virginia creeper that hang between boldly carved and painted oak posts. A large bronze sculpture of a boy with a heron overlooks four small fountains and a swirling box-hedge parterre.

A series of grass terraces with panoramic views leads from one site to the next. You'll see a magnificent ancient great white oak, the largest tree on the estate, on the Oak Lawn below a steep hillside—apparently a favorite picnic site of the Choates; a "Rond Point," enclosed by carefully clipped hedges, where theatrical skits took place; a shady, mossy Linden Walk, inspired by the romantic allées Miss Choate saw in Germany; a tree peony terrace with dozens of these glorious plants featuring giant blossoms in the prettiest warm shades; an arborvitae walk; and a formal allée of clipped arborvitae in symmetrical precision, maintained from the original gardens. There is a walled Chinese Garden (Steele's last effort at Naumkeag), including a Chinese-style temple with a brilliant blue tile roof circled by a group of ginko trees, mossy rocks, and Buddahs, lions, and other objects collected by Miss Choate in her travels; it is entered through a traditional circular moon gate within a curving brick and stone wall, which is in itself a work of art. Not unexpectedly, there is a rose garden too, but this is hardly your traditional example. View it from a railed terrace above, where its serpentine shapes appear before you like an abstract painting, its delicate arabesques of gravel winding through sixteen beds of floribunda roses.

The most innovative feature at Naumkeag, the famous Blue Steps, came about for the most practical of reasons. Because the wooded slope from the Afternoon Garden to Miss Choate's kitchen garden and greenhouses were too steep for her to negotiate with ease, she told Steele "he must make me some steps that would be both convenient and easy. . . ." As she later said, "Little did I realize what I was in for." The extraordinary design features a descending series of delicate concrete arches, with a double flight of cement steps painted the same blue as the posts in the Afternoon Garden; water descends in a channel through them, trickling down from a water tunnel connecting the fountains of the Afternoon Garden above. Surrounding the steps on each side is a thick stand of white birches, reflecting the same brilliant white as the sweeping painted railing of the steps. To appreciate this truly avant-garde design, you must look up from the terrace below the steps.

Naumkeag, which was bequeathed to the Trustees of Reservations after Miss Choate's death in 1958, remains a tribute to the collaborative efforts of a great landscape designer and a very determined gardener. Try to visit on a weekday, when you're more likely to experience the same peace and quiet Miss Choate did, many years ago.

❀ **Admission:** Fee.

Garden open: The house and gardens are open daily 10:00 A.M. to 5:00 P.M. from Memorial Day weekend to Columbus Day.

Further information: Tours of the house with an introduction to the gardens are offered, or you can walk through the gardens at will, using the complimentary map.

Directions: From Boston, take I–90 (Massachusetts Turnpike) to exit B3, to Route 22; go about 1 mile to Route 102 to Stockbridge. From the intersections of Routes 7 and 102 (at the Red Lion Inn), take Pine

Street north; bear left on Prospect Hill. You will find Naumkeag's gate about ½ mile on the left.

12. The Vale, the Lyman Estate

185 Lyman Street, **Waltham**, MA, (781) 891–1985
www.spnea.org/visit/land/mass.html

*W*E OFTEN associate with England the very idea of the eighteenth- and early nineteenth-century American country estate, with its sweeping expanse of lawns, serpentine paths, and profusion of flower gardens. The Vale, the estate of Theodore Lyman not far from Boston, was designed (and has been restored) in the English naturalistic style. This is a beautiful thirty-acre site with a fine house, terrific greenhouses, and a delectable garden, and we found it to be one of the most appealing such places we have seen.

Built in 1793 by Lyman, a wealthy Boston merchant with a taste in horticulture, the Vale was designed to be a self-sufficient country estate for summer use. The fine, very large white manor house was designed by Samuel McIntire and is open to the public. The magnificent property (once 550 acres) included rolling farm fields, an ornamental pond, woodlands, a deer park, naturalistic flower gardens, and five greenhouses. (One of the greenhouses here is said to be the oldest standing greenhouse in the nation; it was once heated with a Dutch stove.) The property—diminished in size but still beautiful and in the same family's hands—was given to the Society for the Preservation of New England Antiquities in 1952. It is also a National Historic Landmark.

The landscape design of the Vale emphasizes the informal, the pleasingly irregular and free-form patterns of the naturalistic style. Winding paths and nearby woods (celebrating "the American Wilderness") are part of the design. There are few rectangular flower beds here, nor will you find topiary or boxwood hedges emphasizing long, straight lines. Instead the focal point of the flower gardens near the mansion is a wonderful long, high, curving brick wall that provides the backdrop to a spectacular display of flowers. This huge cultivated area for flowers has been restored in a similarly informal way, with what is known as an English garden; it is without doubt among the most luscious we have seen.

Here you'll find wisteria vines and roses forming a backdrop on the brick wall, and huge clumps of both flowering shrubs and perennial blooms harmoniously interspersed with one another. There is hardly a bit of space between these plantings, giving the impression of an overgrown—but perfectly kept—garden. Small fruit trees, peonies, and iris, in glorious shades of lavender and violet, are mingled with lamb's ears with their pale grey-green leaves and the delicate pinks and feathery white of flowering shrubs. Two small summerhouses complement the wall and its garden: The elegant templelike structure at the end of the wall originally was part of the front entrance of the house.

In keeping with the serpentine design of this flower bed is a display of rhododendrons across the lawn that has been allowed to grow into an informal wall of its own. Colors of the flowers range from the deepest rose to bright orange.

A path will take you to the greenhouses. Lyman was not alone in his passion for growing exotic plants. He raised pineapples, bananas, and oranges—you can see such fruit in the greenhouses today. The Grape House, with its impeccably lineaged vines, includes cuttings from Germany and Hampton Court, England. American horticulturalists were wild about camellias, first brought from Asia to the West in 1797. You can visit the Camellia House built in 1820; it is particularly lovely in late winter. One greenhouse is used to provide flowers for the house and for sale to help support the Vale. If you like greenhouses with their warm, perfumed profusion of exotic plants, you will certainly like these examples.

A visit to this estate provides a variety of garden experiences; we found it to be quiet and uncrowded (we were there during the week) and thoroughly enjoyable whether you are in the greenhouses, walking across the great lawns, or relishing the brilliant colors and shapes of the flowers by the wall.

❄ **Admission:** Free.

Garden open: The grounds of the Lyman Estate are open all of the time; the greenhouses are open 9:00 A.M. to 3:00 P.M. Monday through Saturday.

Further information: Tours are available, and the house is open for group tours by appointment.

Directions: Waltham is north of Boston. From Route 20 (which is North Beacon Street, and then Main Street), turn onto Lyman Street and follow signs to the corner of Beaver Street.

13. Stanley Park

400 Western Avenue, **Westfield,** MA, www.stanleypark.org

$\mathcal{S}$TANLEY PARK is a choice example of what a public park can be with imagination and care: Not only is this 275-acre site at the foothills of the Berkshires unusually well designed, but it is impeccably maintained—something of a rarity these days. Its prize gardens, wildlife sanctuary, reflecting ponds, brooks, delicate waterfalls, arboretum, wooded trails, and recreation fields provide a serene environment for walkers, gardeners, nature lovers, and families out for a picnic amid the greenery. The park even serves as a cultural resource in the community, offering summer concerts (including carillon performances from its one-of-a-kind Carillon Tower), arts festivals, and garden workshops. Definitely not your standard park fare!

For us Stanley Park was particularly inviting as a landscape. Our first impression, as we walked down its shady slopes (the terrain here is mildly hilly), was of being on a movie set, with one picture-perfect scene flowing into the next—and with the sounds of rippling, cascading, and rushing water adding to the bucolic ambience. One tableau reminded us somewhat of a Swiss landscape, complete with hillside, picturesque covered bridge, pristine pond, and gliding swans and ducks. Actually a part of the so-called Colonial Pond Area, it became more recognizable as the early American setting it's supposed to represent, once the delightful herb garden and orchard, working mill and waterwheel, old town meetinghouse, carriage shed, and blacksmith shop all came in view. (Children will be particularly intrigued by the latter, which has an operating forge, bellows, and anvil.) Fortunately, these historic replicas—unlike many we have seen— are tasteful, and not in the least overdone.

A small path alongside a canal leads to the Japanese garden, a particularly graceful interpretation of this style. Here the requisite Tea House is surrounded by flowering azaleas and rhododendrons (quite a sight in May and June); arched bridges, stone statuary, and rock gardens with delicate miniature evergreens complete the scene.

You can explore the park's many garden pleasures on your own, as you meander along grassy paths and stone walkways from one to the next. Among them: the rhododendron display garden (hundreds of species), herb and perennial display gardens (culinary, medicinal, fragrant varieties), the American Wildflower Society Display Garden (at its most glorious in May and June), and the five-acre arboretum.

But best of all is the lovely rose garden. Situated alongside the Carillon Tower, it is formally known as the All-America Rose Selection, Inc., Public Rose Garden, and has won prestigious awards. You can walk amid the 2,500 rose bushes (at least fifty varieties), taking in the magnificent annual and perennial beds nearby. These are carefully laid out in luscious, colorful patterns and complement the rose garden's delicacy. Both are at their height from June to September.

Stanley Park was the creation of Frank Stanley Beveridge, a forward-thinking entrepreneur and public-spirited individual whose boyhood dream apparently was to build such a public place for everyone's pleasure. Luckily his vision became reality, and in 1949 the park became a charitable corporation to ensure its upkeep for future generations.

We were told that some 250,000 visitors enjoy these vast grounds annually, something that would no doubt please Mr. Beveridge. But while we were there (granted, on a weekday), we saw few others and had the place almost to ourselves—which pleased us!

❀ **Admission:** All facilities and programs are free (except some of the summer concerts).

Garden open: The park is open 8:00 A.M. to dusk from Mother's Day to Columbus Day weekend (some of the recreational facilities are open year-round).

Further information: Accessible to disabled people.

Directions: From I–90 (the Massachusetts Turnpike), take exit 3 into Westfield; at the rotary take Court Street west, which becomes Western Avenue. The park is located at the intersection of Kensington (make a left).

Don't Miss . . .

14. Isabella Stewart Gardner Museum

280 The Fenway, **Boston,** MA, (617) 566–1401
www.gardnermuseum.org

A VISIT TO this venerable museum is a real treat for those interested both in fine art and enclosed gardens. The elegant Venetian-style palazzo features an exceptional art collection known the world over. In the center is a truly magnificent courtyard with rare and beautiful plants. This is the exquisite setting for many year-round chamber music concerts and special garden displays.

❀ **Admission:** Fee.

Garden open: Tuesday through Sunday 11:00 A.M. to 5:00 P.M.

15. Newbury Perennial Gardens

65 Orchard Street, **Byfield,** MA, (508) 462–1144
www.newburyperennialgardens.com

THERE ARE TWENTY display gardens across a large estate here as well as a commercial nursery business. The pretty rolling green terrain was once a "ragged hayfield." The owner has transformed it into a series of elegant gardens focusing on color and texture that fit nicely into the landscape behind his house. There are a variety of lovely (and some very unusual) types of gardens: a weeping garden; a spectacular shrub border garden that blooms throughout the season and is filled with larger perennials and evergreens; a flame garden featuring yellow, orange, and red blooms near a pond with white swans; a white garden; an island garden that peaks in June with lupines, peonies, and poppies; a heather garden in delicious shades of gray-greens, yellows, and oranges; hosta and daylily collections; a bog garden; and a newly constructed grotto garden. These are just a few of the interesting sights here.

You will enjoy walking around these thematic plantings, and for any visiting gardener who lives in a fairly cold northern clime like this one in northern Massachusetts, this is a good place to come and see what can be accomplished. (For example, there is a type of azalea that deer do not touch!) You can either get a self-guiding map and go around by yourself, or you can request (in advance) a tour from the welcoming and knowledgeable owner.

❁ **Admission:** Fee.
Garden open: Mid-April to September.

16. Longfellow House

105 Brattle Street, **Cambridge,** MA, (617) 876–4491
www.nps.gov/long

This National Historic Site, graciously set on one of the most distinguished and beautiful streets in Cambridge, is where Longfellow lived with his family from 1837 until his death in 1882. The elegant house overlooks terraced lawns, brick walkways, large shade trees, lilac bushes, and a delightful enclosed formal garden designed by the poet himself.

You can visit the house and learn about its long history and memorabilia. It was built in 1759 for John Vassall, a young Tory, and later served as George Washington's headquarters. Longfellow lived here as a lodger until his future father-in-law gave the house as a wedding gift to the young couple.

The lovely, peaceful grounds can be enjoyed at will or by guided tour. The garden Longfellow laid out in 1845 has been faithfully restored according to his original design. You enter it through a lattice fence behind the house, walking along winding gravel paths. Colorful arabesque-shape flower beds of iris, peonies, tulips, and other perennials form decorative patterns within clipped low boxwood hedges. Square corner beds of phlox, marguerites, and heliotrope define the outside edges of the garden. In the center is a decorative sundial. Beyond this charming garden is a wide lawn with fine specimen trees. You won't find the famous chestnut tree immortalized by Longfellow's verse—it was cut down long ago and, in fact, was not precisely here to begin with—but there are other trees that are equally spreading, nonetheless.

❀ **Admission:** Free.

Garden open: Daily. The house is open 10:00 A.M. to 4:30 P.M. Wednesday through Sunday. There are several tours daily.

17. Mount Auburn Cemetery

580 Mount Auburn Street, **Cambridge,** MA, (617) 547–7105

THIS VENERABLE nineteenth-century cemetery, the country's first "garden" cemetery, was in fact founded by a group of horticultural-ists. In these 172 acres you are surrounded by a sweeping landscape of manicured lawns and ornamental trees and shrubs adorning the grave sites. Many of these are elaborate Victorian monuments and Greek-like temples (some designed by noted sculptors, such as Augustus Saint-Gaudens). Winslow Homer, Mary Baker Eddy, Henry Wadsworth Longfellow, and Oliver Wendell Holmes are among the well-known Americans buried here.

The cemetery is a special delight in spring, when dogwoods, Japanese cherries, azaleas, and other flowering plants come into full bloom. In the vast grounds are more than five thousand plant specimens, representing almost six hundred different species (you'll find wonderful examples in the greenhouse). Energetic visitors should climb the 60-foot tower for a panoramic view of the ceme-tery and Boston. The cemetery offers walking tours, lectures, and other activities.

❀ **Admission:** Free.

Garden open: Daily 8:00 A.M. to dusk.

18. Beauport, the Sleeper McCann House

75 Eastern Point Boulevard, **Gloucester,** MA, (978) 283–0800
www.spnea.org/visit/homes/beauport.html

THIS SPECTACULARLY SET forty-room house (filled with early American antiques and oddities) can truly be called "waterside." Its site is right on the edge of Gloucester Harbor, overlooking the town, the docks, the boats, and the sea. Beauport was constructed beginning in 1907 (and continuing for twenty-seven years) by a prominent interior designer and collector named Henry Davis Sleeper. (Among his clients were such Hollywood luminaries as Joan Crawford and Fredric March; he also built a house for Henry Francis Du Pont, whose Winterthur in Delaware was related in design. He had a taste for the intimate and cozy rather than the grand and palatial.)

The style of the house—with dormers, turrets, intimate interiors, and colored glass in the windows—was much admired in its day, and a similar intimate taste prevails in the gardens. Surprisingly green for such a beachfront setting, these small spaces are also designed as a series of intimate rooms. The gardens nestle into each level of a central area created by the different wings of the house. They are divided by little grassy paths and stone steps.

❀ **Admission:** Fee.
Garden open: Mid-May to mid-October.

19. Hammond Castle

Hesperus Avenue, **Gloucester,** MA, (978) 283–2080
www.hammondcastle.org

HAMMOND CASTLE evokes the romance of a distant past, resembling a medieval fortress complete with massive stone towers, drawbridge, and flying buttresses. Spectacularly set atop the rocky cliffs of the Atlantic coastline, it is a vision from a Gothic tale. Its gardens are—not surprisingly—unlike those of most other 1920s estates. To reach the castle, you descend along a fairly steep slope of stone walls and boulders surrounded by green and colorful plantings. This is not a traditional rock garden of low and delicate alpine plants carefully nestled amid the rockery; here the scene is more dramatic, befitting the site. Waving about in the ocean breezes are tall flowers (mostly perennials) and willowy greens, set between the huge stones. The combination of sea air, brilliant blossoms, and looming castle with its magnificent ocean views is irresistible.

John Hays Hammond Jr., a prolific inventor and eccentric, built his home between 1926 and 1929. A music lover (in addition to many other things), he installed in the cavernous Great Hall an extraordinary organ of eight thousand pipes. You can visit the castle today (by guided tour) and marvel at this amazing instrument, along with numerous other eclectic furnishings found throughout. But, mainly, walk around these incredible (though not extensive) grounds and enjoy picturesque views through Gothic arches. As you might expect, this is a prime spot for weddings and other functions.

❀ **Admission:** Fee to visit the castle, but none for the gardens.
Garden open: Daily except during functions (call first).

20. Arnold Arboretum

The Arborway, **Jamaica Plain**, MA, (617) 524–1717
www.arboretum.harvard.edu

THIS IMPORTANT and famous 265-acre arboretum was founded in 1872. Administered by Harvard University, it is a true learning center with plants from all over the world, research greenhouses, and thousands of glorious varieties of trees and shrubs. A walk here, particularly in May and June, is most appealing. There are fine collections of dwarf conifers and bonsai and a delightful Chinese Walk with worldwide plants.

❀ **Admission:** Free.
Garden open: Daily, all day, but check on greenhouse hours.

21. October Mountain State Forest

Woodlawn Road (headquarters), **Lee**, MA, (413) 243-1778

THIS VAST FOREST, one of the state's largest, includes almost 16,000 acres of rugged terrain along the Hoosac Range. The elevations are high (some areas reaching 2,000 feet), the woods are dense, and there are many streams, ponds, rocky outcrops, and gorges. In the midst of these scenic wonders are a wide variety of trees and flowering shrubs, as well as seasonal wildflowers—bloodroot, jack-in-the-pulpit, lilies, lady's slipper, trillium, and more. Especially recommended in May and June, when everything is in full bloom.

❀ **Admission:** Fee in season.
Garden open: Year-round.

22. Jeremiah Lee Mansion Gardens

161 Washington Street, **Marblehead**, MA, (781) 631-1069

THESE LOVELY historic gardens surround the elegant Georgian house that was built for Col. Jeremiah Lee and his family in 1768. Recently restored by the Marblehead Garden Club (after meticulous research on eighteenth-century New England gardens), they feature a sundial garden, an herb garden with geometric design, and a sunken garden with shrubs, trees, and wildflowers. In springtime the gardens are a paradise of blooming azaleas, rhododendrons, lilacs, dogwoods, and bulb flowers; in summer you can enjoy such delights as daylilies, hollyhocks, phlox, peonies, and roses.

❀ **Admission:** Fee.
Garden open: Monday through Saturday, 10:00 A.M. to 4:00 P.M., Sunday noon to 4:00 P.M., from June through October.

23. Maudslay State Park

Off Route 110, **Newburyport**, MA, (978) 465-7223

WITHIN THIS delightful park—a former estate picturesquely situated along the Merrimack River—is the Merrimack River Trail, especially recommended for garden lovers. Here you'll discover magnificent gardens and grounds that were designed by Martha Brooks Hutcheson, one of the first women landscape architects, and her partner, Charles Sprague Sargeant. The trail takes about an hour and a half of leisurely walking and is a delight. The park offers special events in season.

❁ **Admission:** Fee in season.
Garden open: Daily 8:00 A.M. until dusk.

24. Hancock Shaker Village

Junction of Routes 20 and 41, **Pittsfield,** MA
(413) 443–0188
www.hancockshakervillage.org

A HISTORIC eighteenth- and nineteenth-century Shaker community here has fine buildings and extensive gardens, including a vast flower garden, herb garden, and vegetable gardens.

❁ **Admission:** Fee.
Garden open: Seasonally.

25. Pleasant Valley Wildlife Sanctuary

West Dugway Road, **Pittsfield,** MA, (413) 637–0320

THIS 730-ACRE sanctuary is filled with birds, waterfowl, and other wildlife attracted to its wildflowers, ponds, waterways, meadows, and woods. There are 7 miles of trails (some quite rugged and steep), including the Trail of Ledges, leading to a fire tower with broad vistas. Don't miss the museum, which describes it all, including the rich plant life that grows here.

❁ **Admission:** Fee.
Garden open: Sanctuary is open year-round; museum is open from Memorial Day to Labor Day.

26. Parker River National Wildlife Refuge

Plum Island, MA, (978) 465–5753

ON THIS LITTLE island off the coast of Newburyport is one of the prettiest wildlife refuges we've experienced. Its nearly five thousand acres include 6 miles of barrier beach (popular with summer visitors), along with dunes, fresh and saltwater marshes, pools, and woodlands, with a wealth of vegetation. Along a 2-mile nature trail in back of the beach, you can see blueberry, pin and black cherry, woodbine, honeysuckle, beach plum, cranberry, winterberry, wild rose, spirea, and many other plants. Among the refuge's many offerings are plum and cranberry for picking in September and October, boating (in specified areas), fishing, hiking (best after the crowds have gone!), and, of course, year-round bird-watching. Visit the headquarters for more information.

❀ **Admission:** Fee.
Garden open: Year-round.

27. Adams National Historic Site

135 Adams Street, **Quincy,** MA, (617) 770–1175
www.nps.gov/adam

THIS 1731 HOUSE and garden have been home to generations of the accomplished and illustrious Adams family. The gardens combine traditional flower beds that surround elegant walkways with fine trees and plants, some quite old. You can visit the gardens on your own, but you must take a guided tour to see the house.

❀ **Admission:** Fee.
Garden open: Daily mid-April to mid-November.

28. Heritage Museums and Gardens

Pine and Grove Streets, **Sandwich,** MA, (508) 888–3300
www.heritagemuseumsandgardens.org

THIS SEVENTY-SIX-ACRE complex includes a museum of Americana (vintage automobiles, antique lithographs, tools, dolls, and much more) surrounded by nature trails and woodlands. Of special interest to us is the remarkable collection of rhododendrons found here; between 1921 and 1943 the estate belonged to Charles O. Dexter, a noted rhododendron hybridizer. Be sure to enjoy these 35,000 (at last count) examples when they are in full bloom during May and June. The grounds also include 550 varieties of daylilies, as well as many kinds of trees and shrubs interspersed throughout the wooded landscape.

❀ **Admission:** Fee.
Garden open: Monday through Saturday 9:00 A.M. to 6:00 P.M., Sunday noon to 6:00 P.M.

29. Butler Sculpture Park

Shunpike Road, **Sheffield,** MA, (413) 229–8924

THIS HILLTOP sculpture park with panoramic views of the Berkshires is the home of sculptor Robert Butler. His park contains his contemporary, abstract works.

❀ **Admission:** Free.
Garden open: May through October. Call for hours.

30. Bridge of Flowers

Water Street, **Shelburne Falls,** MA, (413) 625–2523

THIS OLD ARCHED trolley bridge has been converted into a 400-foot-long flowering walkway, with luxuriant blooms all along the perimeters and even hanging down the sides—a very pretty sight to see.

✿ **Admission:** Free.
   Garden open: Seasonally.

31. Ipswich River Sanctuary

Topsfield, MA, (978) 887–9264

A FORMER ESTATE, this 1,217-acre site overlooking the Ipswich River has a wealth of flora and fauna. Among its many offerings are its arboretum dating from the early 1900s; it is not only impressive for its exotic specimens—Japanese andromedas, Amur corktree, Oriental photinia, among many others—but also for its magnificent boulders. In spring the wildflower garden is a joy, filled with all the regional species you can think of. The sanctuary, run by the Massachussetts Audubon Society, is also noted for its wide variety of birds. Exhaustive listings of these, as well as other species and plants (more than four hundred), are available at the headquarters.

✿ **Admission:** Fee.
   Garden open: Daily (except Monday) from dawn to dusk. Headquarters is open 9:00 A.M. to 4:00 P.M.

32. Butterfly Place

120 Tyngsboro Road, **Westford,** MA, (978) 392–0955
www.butterflyplace-ma.com

THIS IS A GLASS building with the kinds of flowers growing in it that attract hundreds of living butterflies, a beautiful sight, and educational too.

✿ **Admission:** Fee.
   Garden open: Valentine's Day to early fall.

Gardenwalks in New Hampshire

I frequently tramped eight or ten miles through the deepest snow to keep an appointment with a beechtree, or a yellow birch, or an old acquaintance among the pines.

—Henry David Thoreau

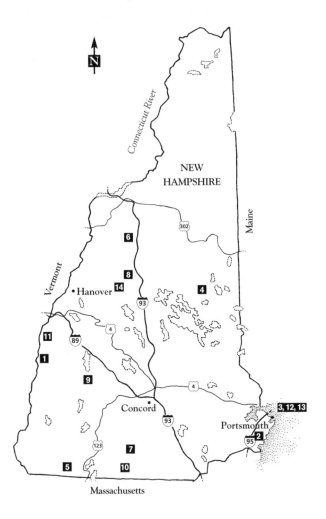

1. Cornish: Aspet, Home and Garden of Augustus Saint-Gaudens
2. North Hampton: Fuller Gardens
3. Portsmouth: Moffatt-Ladd House and Garden

Don't Miss . . .

4. Center Ossipee: Ossipee Lake and Heath Pond Bog
5. Fitzwilliam: Rhododendron State Park
6. Franconia: Bungay Jar Bed and Breakfast

7. Hillsborough: Fox Forest
8. Kinsman Notch: Lost River Nature Garden
9. Newbury: The Fells, John Hay National Wildlife Refuge
10. New Ipswich: Barrett House
11. Plainfield: Plainfield Wildflower Sanctuary
12. Portsmouth: Prescott Park
13. Portsmouth: Strawbery Banke
14. Rumney: Mr. Jacquith's Garden

1. Aspet, Home and Garden of Augustus Saint-Gaudens

Route 12A, **Cornish,** NH, (603) 675–2175
www.sgnhs.org/saga.html

*J*F YOUR IDEA of the nineteenth-century artist living in the depths of a city in a dreadful bohemian garret needs changing, visit the home and garden of Augustus Saint-Gaudens. Now a National Historic Site complete with park rangers and one of the most beautiful landscapes imaginable, Aspet, the artist's summer place and eventual year-round home, is a rarely visited treasure. You may come away thinking that life as one of America's most famous sculptors may have been heavenly.

The National Park Service has made this memorial to Saint-Gaudens an elegant, tasteful, and fascinating place to visit. Though Saint-Gaudens's own experiences there were not so universally glamorous and moneyed as they now appear (the docent told us that several disastrous studio fires and a $30,000 loan to keep the place going were among the less glorious facts of Aspet's past), this estate shows off his art and architecture and garden landscape in a noble fashion. From the distant vistas of fields and mountains, to the charmingly columned and arbored studios, to the delicately set sculptures along garden paths, this is how we would like to imagine an illustrious artist's estate.

The site of Aspet is in rural Cornish, New Hampshire, just beyond the longest covered bridge in the nation. It crosses the Connecticut River from Vermont at Windsor. Nearby, a perfectly kept roadway into the deep woods takes you to Aspet. It was here that the artist discovered an old New England inn set amid a poetic, wild landscape with ravines, waterfall, glorious vistas, and romantic light.

The house and surroundings seemed to us wonderfully remote, like some Shangri-la amid the picturesque New England countryside. The 150-acre property includes the sculptor's home (the original inn); several studios; formal gardens; a deep, wooded ravine; and enough informal garden areas, fields, and lawns to satisfy even a walker without a taste for sculpture. A striking view of nearby Mount Ascutney adds to the vista. Though the art is of course the major attraction of Aspet, the gardens are strikingly lovely, creating an aesthetic and inviting surrounding for outdoor sculpture. Augustus Saint-Gaudens was one of America's premier artists and probably its most beloved nineteenth-century sculptor. His naturalistic approach contrasted with the smooth, controlled surfaces and contours of neoclassical sculpture that had been in vogue. By 1880 he had become an acknowledged leader of American sculptors in an era in which the memorial statue was a necessity in every city square. Other artists joined him in rejecting academicism; they sought to free both painting and sculpture from academic and banal styles of portraiture.

His commemorative statues of famous people (including Abraham Lincoln) were in great demand and are familiar images to us today. But perhaps his best-known and most beloved work—beautifully displayed at Aspet—was his venture into a more emotional style: his Adams Memorial. This grieving, hooded figure was arguably the most original and haunting sculpture yet achieved by an American.

Saint-Gaudens became a widely respected teacher and leader of other artists. In 1885, after he bought the old staging inn that was to become Aspet, Cornish became the center of an artists' colony that grew up about him. (Legend has it that a friend persuaded him to go to New England in the summertime; he was then at work on an important Lincoln portrait and was told that he would find among the natives of New Hampshire many "Lincoln-shaped" men to use for models.) Aspet became a center both for sculptors and other creative people; Saint-Gaudens's salon attracted poets, novelists, journalists, and actors. Summer visitors and art colony residents and their colleagues were noted in the fields of architecture, landscape, and garden design. Among them were Charles Platt, who wrote the first treatise in America on Italianate gardens; the illustrator Maxfield Parrish, whose paintings appeared in Edith Wharton's 1904 publication *Italian Villas and Their Gardens;* architects Stanford White and George Babb; and Saint-Gaudens's own niece, Rose Standish Nichols, a designer of gardens.

It was Babb (an associate of Stanford White) who designed the columned veranda of the house and turned the old hay barn into the delightful Italianate Little Studio. In fact, a classical style reminiscent of ancient Roman villas pervades many of the architectural and garden sites of Aspet; there are colonnades and porticos, picturesque gates and vine-covered pergolas, as well as formally designed plantings.

Saint-Gaudens took a personal interest in the design of the gardens; he had studied French and Italian landscape design for years and favored a strong architectural layout for the formal gardens. He planted hemlock and pine hedges to enclose each area, creating what might be termed garden rooms. Within each such area, he laid out terraces and flower beds, geometrically designed paths, central fountains, and statues, of course. There are statues everywhere. Small sculptured heads appear above the boxwood here and there. There are pools, fountains that shoot jets of water through the mouths of fish and turtles (designed by the sculptor), and marble benches for the proper contemplation of it all. (The white bench decorated with figures of Pan playing his pipes is, however, the work of Augustus's brother Louis, also a sculptor of note.) These Italianate gardens are filled with "old-fashioned" perennials and colorful annuals; the overall effect is of a romantic profusion of flowers amid very orderly settings.

Saint-Gaudens also liked games and sports. There is a lawn-bowling green in the middle of one garden area, and there are bridle paths, a toboggan run, a swimming hole, and numerous hiking trails on the property. By combining his love of art, sport, formal gardens, and natural scenery, the sculptor sought at Aspet to create a total environment that reflected his view of the best of the American spirit. With its references to classical as well as romantic styles, Saint-Gaudens's Aspet represented a particularly nineteenth-century American vision.

The gardens are on three levels. You may walk around them informally (though the house visit requires a tour). From the upper level (where you exit from the veranda of the house), you take a small flight of brick steps, passing through a trellised pergola, along a path edged with carefully trimmed giant yew spheres.

You arrive at the middle terrace, which contains formal flower beds—outlined in century-old hedges of clipped eastern white pine. These densely blooming, cottage-style gardens have a particularly bright and tall feeling: hollyhocks, glads, daylilies, snapdragons, bachelor's buttons, iris—among other old-fashioned favorites—are gaily massed together. In the center is a delicate statue of Hermes, rising above the waving flowers.

On the lower level, you'll find the Little Studio, a delightful Italianate classical structure whose brilliant white columns are ornamented with clinging vines that contrast with a rose-red wall ("Pompeiian red") and a frieze that copies the Parthenon. (Don't miss seeing the inside of this studio.) Adjoining the Little Studio is one of the most enchanting gardens of all: Here, bordered by startling white birches and pine hedges is another garden room. The rectangular area is planted with perennials and divided by pathways, including one that leads to a white wooden bench at the end. Its carvings represent the four seasons. Also in this very charming spot is a delicate water garden, with a reflecting pool featuring a classical statue of Pan playing his pipes and small sculpted animals shooting gentle jets of water through their mouths.

On leaving this area, follow the path toward the Adams Memorial, in its own garden. Arguably Saint-Gaudens's most stunning work, the shrouded, seated figure was commissioned by Henry Adams on the death of his wife in 1885. Not a portrait, but a striking symbol of mourning, the Adams Memorial brought American sculpture to a new depth of emotion, anticipating expressionism by many years. The statue is surrounded by an enclosing and stately square-cut hedge and elegant plantings.

Through the hedgerow (peopled by small marble heads peeking above the shrubbery) and along the birch-lined pathway, you'll see the bowling green, the carriage barn, and several well-known sculptures. These include a portrait bust of Abraham Lincoln and the Shaw Memorial to the Fifty-fourth Massachusetts Regiment, the first black regiment in the Civil War. It is surrounded by a white-grape arbor in a sun-dappled garden.

Across the open lawn you'll find the Gallery, a comparatively modern building housing some of the artist's major sculpture both indoors (a full-length sculpted portrait of Robert Louis Stevenson) and out (another major work, *The Farragut Base*). There is a reflecting pool here and more gardens in a formal, geometrically arranged style.

The estate also includes a dramatic and rather steep descent into a forested ravine. If you choose to take this walk, you will find it exceptionally beautiful, but be sure you are wearing proper shoes for a climb!

The path eventually will bring you to the bottom of the great field in front of the house where the Cornish art colony had a Greek-style, columned temple (actually a replica of a stage set) erected in 1905 to celebrate twenty years of Saint-Gaudens's residence in Aspet. It became the family burial place.

Certainly one of the most intriguing things about Aspet is the overall design of the landscape, with its winning combination of natural formal elements. With the studio and house areas, the axial paths and lines of sight are carefully accented with marble paths, groves of trees, and formal hedgerows, while all around it the natural beauty of the New England landscape has been magnificently preserved. This is a site well worth visiting for both garden enthusiasts and art lovers.

❀ **Admission:** Fee for persons over sixteen.

Garden open: The Saint-Gaudens National Historic Site is open daily from the last weekend in May through October 31. The buildings are open 8:30 A.M. to 4:40 P.M. and the grounds 8:00 A.M. until dark.

Further information: The mailing address is R.R. 3, Box 73, Cornish, NH 03745.

Directions: From Boston take Interstate 90 (the Massachusetts Turnpike) to Interstate 91 north to exit 8; take Route 131 east and go left onto Route 12A north. Aspet is located just of Route 12A in Cornish; it is 12 miles north of Claremont and 1½ miles north of the covered bridge at Windsor, Vermont.

2. Fuller Gardens

10 Willow Avenue, **North Hampton,** NH, (603) 964-5414
www.fullergardens.org

*J*UST ACROSS the street from the Atlantic Ocean in a neighborhood of great summer mansions, you'll find some surprisingly elegant estate gardens that have nothing to do with beach grasses and wild roses. Fuller Gardens were part of the summer estate of Alvan T. Fuller, a governor of Massachusetts, and they were designed in the 1920s by no less a landscape specialist than Arthur Shurtleff (later known as Shurcliff), with additions in the 1930s by the Olmsted brothers. These extensive formal gardens—divided into several separate parts—are fine examples of the colonial revival style. Though there are a variety of garden attractions here, most people come to see the roses.

The seaside location is apparently ideal for roses, and here you'll find two spectacular rose gardens (as well as a very pretty Japanese garden, profuse perennial beds, and a conservatory of exotic plantings). Some 1,500 rose bushes of all types—grandifloras, floribundas, and hybrid teas—are planted in a variety of geometric beds; in fact, these are among the best-designed rose gardens we have seen anywhere. Rather than the somewhat undistinguished, monolithic rose beds of so many gardens, these have been designed to complement the roses—both in color and texture. (This is, by the way, an official All-America Rose Display Garden for New Hampshire.)

The first of the rose gardens is in an enclosed, squarish garden arranged in geometric patterns with small statues and fountains to ornament the brilliant blooms. It is charming and intimate and enclosed—on one side by a high wooden fence with espaliered apple trees.

The second (behind the Japanese garden) is truly magnificent. In an enormous sunken garden surrounded by very wide, very uniform, waist-high hedges of yew, a series of diamond-shape rose beds are divided by extremely narrow paths. Each bed is filled with a different color and species of rose. Surrounding the hedges are borders of glorious perennials that provide contrast and emphasis. This is an inspired design for the delicate rose!

As you walk around and among the mazelike arrangement of the paths, don't miss the many small decorations that add to the ambience—the Etruscan urns, the planters at the gates overflowing with pretty blossoms, the little statuary almost behind the flowers.

Between these rose gardens is the Japanese garden, a setting of shade and quiet greenery, with the sound of delicately running water and birds singing. Designed by Shurtleff in 1935, it is a haven of darkness and profuse greenery, interspersed with arched bridges and step-ping-stones in great contrast to the bright sunlit rose gardens. This is a Japanese garden without cuteness; it is an oasis of calm and elegance.

There is also a greenhouse with some exotic tropical and desert plantings. In the sheltered lee immediately next to the structure is a series of cold-frame beds of perennials that seem to relish the salty air—such as giant yellow sunflowers.

You will find Fuller Gardens very spiffy—not a blade of grass is out of place, and little is left to chance. These gardens (carefully labeled) are an unexpected treat in such a windy, cold climate. They are less than an hour from Boston, and well worth the trip.

> ❀ **Admission:** Fee.
>
> **Garden open:** Daily 10:00 A.M. to 6:00 P.M. from early May through mid-October.
>
> **Further information:** We recommend visiting during the rose season, though there are thousands of spring bulbs to be enjoyed in May and early June.
>
> **Directions:** From Boston take Interstate 95 north to exit at Route 101 east; go to Route 1A (at the shoreline). Fuller Gardens are located 200 yards north of the junction.

3. Moffatt-Ladd House and Garden

154 Market Street, **Portsmouth,** NH, (603) 436-8221

*C*OLONIAL GARDENS that have been kept up through the years are among the greatest of rarities—far harder to find than well-maintained colonial houses. Judging by the Moffatt-Ladd House garden, a 1½-acre pleasure garden behind the house, such gardens were masterpieces of design and charm. We have seldom seen a more felicitous arrangement of terraces, walkways, flowers, shrubbery, trees, arbors, and even grass steps up and down. This garden shows us what our colonial forebears knew—that the small, well-designed garden can be infinitely more pleasing than the large and formal. Here is a garden to sit in all day!

The Moffatt-Ladd House—a beauty—was built in 1763 in the first style of elegance. The house took 467 days to complete, by the way, and had its own masthouse and wharf across the street on the Piscataqua River. (A counting office adjoining the house was added in the 1830s.) John Moffatt was a successful sea captain, and the house was built as a wedding gift for his son Samuel; it eventually became the home of his granddaughter, Mrs. Alexander Ladd. The property stayed in the family and is now preserved by descendants of the Moffatts and Ladds and the Colonial Dames of America. (This is one house tour we recommend, for the architecture, the craftsmanship of the handcarving, and the fine paintings and furnishings are well worth seeing.)

The garden was laid out behind and to the side of the house in its present design about 150 years ago, following plans and using some plantings that were there before. Alexander Hamilton Ladd, who redid the garden in the mid-nineteenth century, wrote that some of the plants had been put in by his mother and grandmother; two examples survive from the eighteenth century. You'll see a huge horse chestnut tree planted in 1776 (just after a family member had signed the Declaration of Independence), and an English damask rose planted in 1768.

The garden is perfectly kept, but its neatness is not antiseptic; instead, it is a particularly charming garden in its unusual design. Though there are formal plantings on either side of a 300-foot axis from the house to a wrought-iron gate at the end, there are numerous serpentine shapes with winding brick and gravel walkways, surprising trellises including a colonial spiral, and terraces on four levels—the highest reached by rare grass steps cut into the hillside. Other features include a very green lawn separating many small beds planted with the brightest yellow dahlias we have ever seen, as well as feathery cosmos, a trellis of grapes, a great larch tree, a white pergola, beehives, and a new surprise around every bend.

Though not one of the larger gardens in this book, this is one of our favorites. Here you can see how a smallish, hilly plot, enclosed on all sides and in the middle of a cold-climed, northern city, can be quite magically turned into a place of beauty and repose.

❀ **Admission:** Fee.

Garden open: Monday through Saturday 10:00 A.M. to 4:00 P.M. and Sunday 2:00 to 5:00 P.M. from June 15 to October 15, and by special appointment.

Further information: Tours are offered, but the garden can be seen on your own.

Directions: Portsmouth is one hour north of Boston on I–95. Take exit 7 into Portsmouth (Market Street) to number 154.

Don't Miss . . .

4. Ossipee Lake and Heath Pond Bog

Intersection of Routes 16 and 25, **Center Ossipee,** NH

ARE WILD ORCHIDS your special interest? This lovely undeveloped area is a National Natural Landmark; you can walk on a trail around the fragile Heath Pond Bog and see for yourself wild orchids, insectivorous plants, and other wildflowers totally undisturbed.

❀ **Admission:** Free.

Garden open: Visit in season.

5. Rhododendron State Park

Off Route 119, 3 miles to town, **Fitzwilliam,** NH
www.nhstateparks.org/ParksPages/Rhododendron/
Rhododendron.html

THIS IS A sixteen-acre grove of huge rhododendrons, with hiking trails into the thick surrounding forest. Visit in late spring.

❀ **Admission:** Fee.
Garden open: Weekends early May to mid-June, daily mid-June to Labor Day.

6. Bungay Jar Bed and Breakfast

Easton Valley Road, **Franconia**, NH, (800) 421–0701

THIS BEAUTIFULLY SITUATED B&B has a view of the mountains and a lovely rustic garden featuring native plantings, lilacs, fruit trees, perennial gardens, a lily pond, and charming rocky walls and steps. There is also a wildflower meadow with trails to a riverside.

❀ **Admission:** Free.
Garden open: Seasonally.

7. Fox Forest

Route 202, **Hillsborough,** NH

MORE THAN 20 miles of trails cut through this rather rugged terrain. But for those interested in native New England shrubs and trees and ferns, this is not to be missed. Here you'll find a treasure trove of specimens from witch hazel and shadbush trees to wild plum and dogwood. Pick up plant lists before you start out.

❀ **Admission:** Free.
Garden open: Seasonally.

8. Lost River Nature Garden

Route 112, 6 miles west of North Woodstock
Kinsman Notch, NH, www.findlostriver.com

HERE, AMID the glacial caverns and giant potholes and the Gorge at Paradise Falls, you'll find some three hundred labeled varieties of native flowering plants, as well as ferns and mosses. Visit between June and September.

✺ **Admission:** Free.
Garden open: Mid-May to mid-October.

9. The Fells, John Hay National Wildlife Refuge

Route 103A, **Newbury,** NH, (603) 763–4789, www.thefells.org

WITHIN THIS GREAT refuge you'll find a surprising series of fine gardens, as well as the historic Hay house, forests, trails, and sweeping green lawns. Of particular interest is the rock garden, one of the best and largest in New England. Its peak seasons are June and July and "foliage" in October—like the surrounding mountain scenery. Just as the autumn leaves change color, plants in the garden too turn to brilliant shades of red. There are also a walled woodland garden and a 100-foot-long perennial border, at its height in midsummer with pinks and blues and whites. A spectacular collection of lilacs, azaleas, and rhododendrons is best seen in late spring and early summer.

✺ **Admission:** Free.
Garden open: Seasonally; hiking trails open year-round.

10. Barrett House

79 Main Street, **New Ipswich,** NH, (603) 878–2517
www.spnea.org/visit/homes/barrett.html

THOUGH MORE A landscape than a garden of flowers, Barrett House grounds are a picturesque and evocative place to visit. Here, where *The Europeans* was filmed, are nearly one hundred acres of meadowlands and forest with a broad, grassy, terraced walkway through the woods to an idyllic, lacy Gothic revival gazebo. The imposing house and grounds are open for tours.

✤ **Admission:** Fee.
Garden open: June 1 to October 15.

11. Plainfield Wildflower Sanctuary

River Road off Route 12A, **Plainfield,** NH, www.newfs.org

ALONG THE Connecticut River is this slope, field, and riverbank of wildflowers and ferns. It is maintained by the New England Wild Flower Society. Visit in spring and summer.

✤ **Admission:** Free.
Garden open: Seasonally.

12. Prescott Park

Marcy Street, **Portsmouth,** NH
www.portsmouthnh.com/visitors/ppark.html

THIS IS without a doubt one of the most beautiful downtown city parks we have seen, not only because of its location right on the water, but because two sisters named Prescott left a legacy of flowers to the city. Every year several extremely large and profusely planted and colorful flower beds are cared for by University of New

Hampshire horticultural students. The plantings—while not particularly unusual—are spectacular in their brilliance; there is even a gate of flowers—impatiens—that grow vertically on the fence.

❀ **Admission:** Free.
Garden open: Seasonally.

13. Strawbery Banke

Marcy Street, **Portsmouth,** NH, (603) 433–1100
www.strawberybanke.org

THIS IS AN entire section of town featuring historic houses, several of which have been carefully restored amid small gardens. If you are visiting Strawbery Banke, note especially the Thomas Baily Aldrich Garden, which was redesigned in about 1907 and is a fine example of colonial revival design; the Sherburne House Garden, a vegetable and herb garden based on original archeological research; the Goodwin Mansion Garden, a Victorian and very charming garden created around the time of the Civil War; and a long perennial walkway through the "Village."

❀ **Admission:** Fee.
Garden open: May 1 to October 31.

14. Mr. Jacquith's Garden

Main Street, **Rumney,** NH

MR. JACQUITH has a beautiful garden right on Main Street in this tiny town. Though it's a private garden, he likes visitors, and you may leave a small donation to help with its upkeep.

❀ **Admission:** Free.
Garden open: Summer only.

Gardenwalks in Rhode Island

It is not necessarily those lands which are the most fertile or most favored that seem to me the happiest, but those in which a long stroke of adaptation between man and his environment has brought out the best qualities of both.

—T. S. Eliot

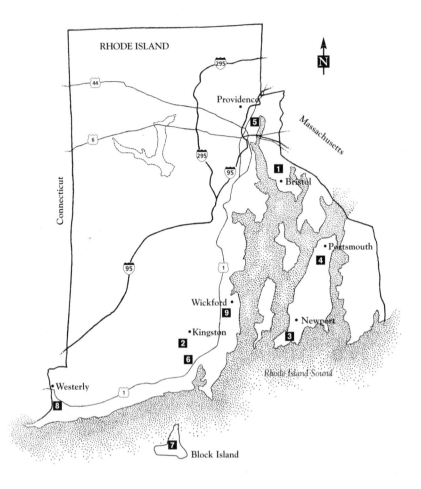

1. Bristol: Blithewold Gardens and Arboretum
2. Kingston: Kinney Azalea Gardens
3. Newport: Hammersmith Farms and Gardens of the Great Mansions
4. Portsmouth: Green Animals
5. Providence: Shakespeare's Head and the Stephen Hopkins House Garden
6. South Kingstown: Ding Hao Garden

Don't Miss . . .

7. Block Island: Rodman's Hollow
8. Westerly: Wilcox Park
9. Wickford: Smith's Castle

1. Blithewold Gardens and Arboretum

101 Ferry Road, **Bristol**, RI, (401) 253–2707, www.blithewold.org

*B*LITHEWOLD means "happy woodlands" in Middle English, and a happy spot this is! The thirty-three-acre estate combines delightful gardens, woodlands, and sweeping lawns idyllically set at water's edge. Walking through these carefully landscaped grounds—enjoying the old-fashioned flower beds, rose arbor, rock and water gardens, enchanting bosquet, and picturesque views overlooking Bristol Harbor and Narragansett Bay—is a joyful experience. The ambience is both gracious and informal, befitting a stylish country house of a bygone era.

In 1894 Augustus Van Wickle, a coal magnate from Pennsylvania, bought Blithewold as a mooring site for the new steam yacht he had just acquired as a surprise gift for his wife. The mansion, surrounded by its romantic waterfront property, became their summer home. To embellish the grounds he hired John De Wolfe, a Brooklyn-based landscape architect. After Van Wickle died suddenly in a hunting accident, De Wolfe continued his work under the guidance of Van Wickle's wife, Bessie. He planted many exotic trees and shrubs that were just being introduced to America from China and Japan. The gardens were nurtured and tended by Marjorie Lyon, the Van Wickles' daughter, until her death at age ninety-three. (Her will stipulated that funds were to be spent first and foremost on the grounds, and only then on the house.)

Today Blithewold is maintained by the Heritage Trust of Rhode Island. The existing seventeenth-century, English-style mansion was built in 1907, after the original house burned down; it can be visited by guided tour. Inside you'll find the many eclectic objects and furnishings Bessie Van Wickle collected on her world travels over the years—from Tiffany lamps and Chinese vases to a mantel from Queen Victoria's nephew's house. But it is in the inviting gardens where you will want to linger most—and at your own pace.

There are seven gardens in all, connected by informal gravel paths and grassy walkways and broad lawns dotted with stone benches: the rose garden, north garden, water and rock gardens, the enclosed garden, cutting and vegetable gardens, and the bosquet. You will find those areas unusually artistic in their color schemes and design. Before setting forth, pick up a walking guide of the grounds (available at the entrance booth), which also indicates the rare plants and trees not to be missed—such as the Japanese tree lilacs and a ninety-year-old giant sequoia, apparently the largest of its kind in the East.

Your first stop is the enclosed rose garden, reached through an arched passageway. Though quite small, it contains several varieties tastefully arranged. Just beyond it is the stone-and-stucco mansion framed by a graceful circular entrance.

The north garden, next to the house (and easily visible from its windows, porches, and brick terrace) is a formal though intimate garden. It consists of perennials—mostly blue and yellow—set around a small pool and fountain.

Next is the bosquet, an airy forest of lush rhododendrons, ferns, carpets of myrtle, and other woodsy delights. In spring its many thousand daffodils add even more enchantment to these "happy woodlands."

A prettily shaded path meanders along, eventually reaching the water and rock gardens. Their picturesque waterside setting makes them especially enticing. Adjacent to one another, they are both inspired by the Japanese style. In the water garden, a weeping willow hangs over two tiny ponds with a connecting arched stone bridge. Wildflowers and grasses surround the garden. The rock garden—literally on the edge of Bristol Harbor—contains many carefully labeled plants artistically set among stones and rocks. Some of the plants are Asian specimens, such as the Japanese anemone. This garden is almost always colorful, with flowering plants blooming from spring through the fall.

At this point you can choose to follow a shoreline path (which will eventually wind around back to the mansion) or continue on your garden tour. The panoramic view overlooking the harbor is irresistible, and you will want to pause and perhaps even put your feet in the water.

The cutting and vegetable gardens are rustic and multicolored. There are beds of poppies, lavender, marigolds, phlox, and other offerings. You are likely to find an army of dedicated volunteers busy at work, picking and weeding. On your right is a wonderfully thick bamboo grove that you can walk through. The bamboo plants, in the softest shade of yellow, move gracefully with the sea breezes.

The last garden to visit is the enclosed garden, an oasis-like, peaceful spot. Surrounded by rhododendrons, hemlocks, and other evergreens, it features many specimen trees of different sizes and shapes—including the previously mentioned giant sequoia. Many of Blithewold's visitors are horticulturalists—amateur or otherwise —and this specimen garden is of great interest to them.

Blithewold is not often crowded; when we last visited on a brillant, late summer day during the week, we had the place almost to ourselves. There are special events during the year (see below), and picnicking, bird-watching, photography, painting, and drawing are permitted on the grounds.

✿ **Admission:** Fee.

Garden open: Daily year-round 10:00 A.M. to 4:00 P.M. The mansion is open 10:00 A.M. to 4:00 P.M. April through October.

Further information: Special events include a Valentine's Day concert, spring bulb display (April), plant sale (May), concerts by the bay in summer, Christmas celebrations, and horticultural and historical programs.

Directions: From Boston take Route 24 to the Mount Hope exit; cross the Mount Hope Bridge, and bear left onto Ferry Road (Route 114). Blithewold is ⅛ mile on the left. From Providence take exit 7 off Interstate 195 east; follow route 114 south through Barrington, Warren, and Bristol to Blithewold.

2. Kinney Azalea Gardens

2391 Kingstown Road, **Kingston,** RI

AN UNEXPECTED and gorgeous surprise in this rocky New England coastal area, these azalea gardens are spectacular in season. And it's a nice long season too—there are so many varieties planted here that the blossoms in this chilly climate near the ocean last from mid-May through the first week of July.

The azaleas are planted over a large woodsy area. There are grassy paths and wonderful rough stone walls (one of our favorite features of the Rhode Island landscape), but the overall feeling is of walking through a natural woodland that just happens to have more than five hundred varieties of the flowering shrubs. Among the varieties—in every color you can think of, except blue—are many rare species, including Geisha azaleas and one hybrid variety that produces both pink and white blossoms simultaneously. Many are glorious in color: deep rose or peach, palest lavender, dark orange. The deciduous varieties in yellow and orange bloom into July. And the azaleas are mixed in with many other woodland pleasures: huge umbrella pines, rhododendrons, pink dogwoods, flourishing leucothoe that drapes over the walls, and numerous forest flowers including trillium, jack-in-the-pulpit, and periwinkle.

The Kinneys are a longtime botanical family. Lorenzo F. Kinney, who started the gardens, was a professor of botany at the university nearby, with a specialty in rhododendrons. Over the years his family and friends turned this into one of the loveliest New England gardens we have seen.

A map is available at the Kinneys' house. This is, by the way, a perfect garden to visit with children in tow, for the rather labyrinthine paths (with some little statuary—pixies for example—hidden here and there) will make it a treat for the younger set. This is not a place where you cannot touch or step. There were many children scampering through the woodsy paths when we visited. And if you come on a Saturday in mid-May, you might be in time for a longtime tradition at the garden's height here: azalea tea!

❀ **Admission:** Donations accepted.

Garden open: Open all summer, but visit in May, June, or early July for best viewing.

Directions: From Interstate 95 take Route 138 east. Pass the University of Rhode Island and turn south on Route 108. Continue on Route 108; you'll find the gardens on your left outside of Kingston. (Also on Route 110, by the way, in late May and early June, you'll find a display of white mountain laurel growing profusely all along the road.)

3. Hammersmith Farm and Gardens of the Great Mansions

Newport, RI, (401) 846–7346 (Hammersmith) and (401) 847–1000 (mansions), www.newportmansions.org

*N*EWPORT, Rhode Island, has a unique place in American history and architecture. On this coastal peninsula, just on the edge of an eighteenth-century fishing and sailing village, some of the greatest mansions of our late nineteenth century were fashioned after French châteaus and mythical castles. The architecture and gardens of Versailles, with their stately elegance and incredible opulence, were of course a major inspiration. In fact, two Newport estates were based on Versailles: Rosecliff was a copy of the Grand Trianon at Versailles, while Marble House imitated the Petit Trianon. The tourist can still visit eight of these palaces of the belle epoque (some were actually called "summer cottages"!) that are as grandiose and lavish as royal residences. They line Bellevue Avenue like great sailing ships behind regal gates and walls.

When these—and many other—grand homes were built by the giants of industry, most of them had elegant gardens to match. Their landscaping and flower gardens were palatial, often patterned on the formal French designs of earlier centuries. But the seaside setting and violent winds and storms of the coastal region made keeping such gardens very difficult. Hurricanes over the years uprooted rare trees, and flower gardens needed constant care and replenishment. Today, though you can visit eight Newport mansions and walk around their extensive grounds, only four have gardens of outstanding interest. (If, however, you enjoy seeing fully these relics of the Gilded Age with or without gardens, a ticket for sale by the Preservation Society, available at any of the great houses, allows you to tour the houses and gardens of all seven of them, except Hammersmith House—which provides its own.)

The most elaborate of the extant Newport gardens is at Hammersmith Farm, the home of Jacqueline Bouvier Kennedy's stepfather, Hugh Auchincloss. This large, shingled, turreted, rather odd-looking mansion is perched over the sea (Narragansett Bay) on the opposite side of the peninsula from the great houses of Bellevue Avenue. The Kennedy wedding reception took place here; the gala event dominated every aspect of a visit to the estate except the gardens. Hammersmith Farm has become somewhat of a tourist attraction, now run by an organization called Camelot Gardens. (You can, however, get a ticket here to see only the grounds.)

When Hammersmith Farms was built (in 1887) on a hill with sloping meadows down to the sea, Frederick Law Olmsted was engaged to design the ninety-seven-acre landscape. The Olmsted design specified formal gardens, allées of trees, a water-lily pool, fountains, sculpture, arched walls and pergolas, and sunken garden beds. The formal garden areas were to be divided by winding paths and more naturalistic areas; Olmsted—as always—wanted his design to conform with the natural beauties of the land rather than to impose upon it.

Over the years the gardens fell into disrepair. After World War II, the Olmsted firm was asked to redesign the gardens in a simpler style. Gardens became lawns and sculpture was stored. (You can see the original gardens in photographs and paintings in the mansion.) Today, in many parts of the estate we see the remains of the original landscape combined with great empty spaces—lawns and fields— where once elaborate gardens bloomed. This juxtaposition of elegant stonework and sunken gardens with emptiness is certainly very odd. But enough has remained of the first Olmsted design to make this an intriguing outing, for what remains seems rather like parts of stage sets for a variety of different dramas.

Begin your tour of the gardens by walking to the north of the house. You will follow along Olmsted's allée of Japanese cedar trees toward the formal gardens. This path will take you to a stone arch, also from the original plan, and to two shorter allées of silver linden trees. Here, in a strikingly empty space, was the huge lily pond, now filled in. Among the several formal flower beds in this section are sets of connected stone arches that nowadays eerily seem to lead nowhere. The sunken beds, however, are filled with colorful plantings and well-kept shrubbery. Opposite, in the woods, other stone arches remain, today covered by overgrown vines. Also in this formal area are a sunken rock garden and an old-fashioned fountain—both remnants of a charming nineteenth-century-style garden. There is a deeply shaded walkway that leads through another stone arch as you head back to the house.

Nearer the house—on the south side, and in view of the blue sea below—is the terraced English flower garden. This recently renovated and luxuriant garden surrounded by stone walls and espaliered pear trees is charming and bright throughout the season. One of the few remaining statues from the Olmsted period is placed at this spot. (Here you may rest on a garden bench under a grape arbor and look out over the expanse of lawn and bay.)

Not far away is an enormous cutting garden of some one hundred varieties; its informality is a nice contrast with the formal gardens to the north. You may also enjoy walking through the well-kept lawns and paths of the estate down to the dock. (The waterfront landscape was used in filming *The Great Gatsby*.)

On the other side of the peninsula, you'll find several gardens of the great houses that are worth a visit. Marble House (1892), designed by Richard Morris Hunt for William Kissam Vanderbilt, was, as we have said, patterned after Versailles's Petit Trianon. Its grounds contain a large, surprising, and brilliantly painted Chinese pagoda set in a carefully designed landscape.

At Rosecliff (1902), designed by Stanford White, you'll find elegant rose gardens in season. The house design included protected terraces on both sides; it is here that the roses grow despite the ocean winds. There are dozens of varieties, including climbing roses along the wall of the mansion. The setting of these five formal beds is spectacular, with ocean waves easily visible beyond the lawn. Graceful statues by Augustus Saint-Gaudens adorn the gardens. The best time to see this garden is July to mid-September.

But our favorite Bellevue Avenue gardens are those of the Elms (1901), a glamorous and somewhat overgrown setting thoroughly reminiscent of eighteenth-century French château gardens. The Elms, designed by Horace Trumbauer, was a copy of the 1750 Château d'Asnières outside Paris, and the gardens capture the ambience and grace of the period. Around the mansion there are numerous rhododendrons, bronze and marble statues, and evergreen shrubbery clipped in topiary shapes. A wisteria balustrade is brilliantly purple in springtime. Great trees, including giant weeping beeches, dot the lawn (but no elms remain). There is a beautiful pathway from the side of the mansion leading to the formal gardens: a mixture of statuary and marble gazebos, busts of mythical figures, and pergolas, fountains, vines, and a formal sunken garden edged in boxwood. The overall impression is delightfully romantic.

Before leaving Newport we recommend the Cliff Walk, which runs along the ocean edge of many of these estates. From here you will have a view not only of the dramatic sea, but of some of the mansions and their gardens.

❀ **Admission:** Fee.

Garden open: Daily April through November.

Further information: Hammersmith Farm is open for guided tours or grounds only, daily from April through mid-November. Newport Preservation Society Mansions (including those described above) are open daily year-round, but to see the gardens we recommend spring, summer, and early fall. They also have special holiday events. (One ticket for all mansions and grounds available, as well as individual houses and combination tickets.)

Directions: To Newport from New York, take I–95 north to exit 3 in Rhode Island to Route 138 east across Jamestown Bridge and across Newport Bridge. For Hammersmith Farm: Once in Newport follow signs to Ocean Drive and Fort Adams State Park. Hammersmith is just beyond the park. Bellevue Avenue is reached by continuing on Ocean Avenue until it intersects with Bellevue.

4. Green Animals

Cory's Lane, **Portsmouth**, RI, (401) 683–1267

*I*F YOU LIKE animal sculptures prettily set along garden paths— and wish to see some whimsical examples that are neither stone nor steel—make a visit to this topiary garden where growing trees and bushes are trimmed into myriad shapes, both abstract and realistic. Green Animals is a small estate whose gardens are filled with members of the animal kingdom, including a giraffe, a giant camel, a bear, a swan, an elephant, a rooster, and even a unicorn, all made of greenery. Set into a formal garden of flowers and hedges and geometric pathways, these cavorting animals are a particular delight to children.

Green Animals, not far from Newport, overlooks Narragansett Bay. It is the oldest topiary garden in the country. The seven-acre estate includes a summerhouse with original furnishings from its nineteenth-century past and a toy collection, but it is particularly the topiary garden that draws visitors.

Green Animals' garden was the idea of a family named Brayton who were enchanted by topiary gardens they had seen in the Azores. They and their gardeners, Joseph Carreiro (a native of the Azores) and his son-in-law, George Medonca, designed the gardens, beginning their work around 1893.

Green Animals' sculptures, made from nature, are both realistic and fanciful. The garden includes about one hundred pieces of topiary art, including geometric shapes, arches and ornamental designs, and some twenty-one animals and birds. The topiary works are made from yew and privet. Other specialties of the garden are thirty-five seasonally planted flower beds in the most perfect condition. There are peach trees and fig trees and grape arbors and various other horticultural pleasures.

In pleasant weather children can sit on tiny animal-shape rocking chairs out among the topiary fantasies. Green Animals is included in a combination ticket with several of the mansions of Newport, or it can be visited separately (at what we thought was an unfortunately rather steep price). If you would enjoy visiting Newport's great houses with their elegant period furnishings and art, however, the combination ticket is well worth the cost.

✿ **Admission:** Fee.
  Garden open: Daily 10:00 A.M. to 5:00 P.M. from May to November.
  Directions: From Providence take I–95 to the Wyoming exit, then follow Route 138 east to Newport. At junction of Routes 138 and 114, take Route 114 and continue for about 7 miles north to Cory's Lane. The garden entrance is on the left.

5. Shakespeare's Head and the Stephen Hopkins House Garden

Meeting Street and Benefit and Hopkins Streets, **Providence**, RI, (401) 831–7440, www.ppsri.org

*T*HESE TWO small but elegant eighteenth-century gardens are within walking distance of one another. Seeing the two gardens on the same outing is both enjoyable and instructive: They provide a glimpse of living history in a notable and charming part of

Providence. In this hilly section of the city, fine eighteenth-century homes of brick and clapboard sit almost immediately next to one another along the narrow streets. (Many of these houses in this historic district bear the names and dates of the original owners.) Tucked into the little spaces between and behind them are their gardens—wonderful examples of what can be accomplished in small urban spaces.

Colonial gardeners knew precisely how to combine practicality with beauty. Within parterres and geometrically designed planting beds, these jewel-size gardens contain both herbs and flowers, brick walls, and boxwood hedges. The restorers of these two gardens were both highly successful in creating a sense of eighteenth-century order and charm; in one case they were able to draw on existing walls and terraces, and in the other on a plan by a descendant of Stephen Hopkins.

The Stephen Hopkins House, built in 1743, is on Benefit Street—a delightful colonial roadway on the hill—at the corner of Hopkins. Stephen Hopkins was a colonial governor of Rhode Island, a chief justice of the superior court, an energetic supporter of colonial rights, and a signer of the Declaration of Independence. His house is open to the public.

About forty years ago, a restoration of the garden was begun by the Dirt Gardeners Club of Providence. They used a design for the garden that was made by Alden Hopkins, a direct descendant of the original owner. He is said to have based his design on gardens at Williamsburg. The gates and entrance to the house are immediately on the street; you enter the garden by descending five steps. A high wall surrounds the property. The parterre garden has geometric beds outlined by low brick walls. In the center is a sundial around which is engraved a quotation by Stephen Hopkins: "A garden that might comfort yield." Despite its small size, the garden does just that.

Not far away, on steep Meeting Street, is the garden of Shakespeare's Head. This rather more elaborate colonial garden is also tiny, but its ingenious use of terraces makes it seem larger. It is part of the property of a historic and interesting house. Built in 1772, the house was the home of the publisher of Providence's first newspaper. The sign at the establishment bore a wood carving of Shakespeare's head as a symbol of literacy—hence the name. In the 1930s the delapidated building was purchased by the Shakespeare's Head Association, restored, and eventually designated a National Historic Landmark.

The garden restoration was begun in 1939 following a plan (based on the excavation of the remains of walls and cobbled areas) by landscape architect James D. Graham. Though there were no plans extant, Graham's idea was to restore the gardens on their three parterre levels, using eighteenth-century historical English-style garden plans, and retaining the brick work from the past. The house is on a steeply sloping street, and the gardens are terraced to conform with the hillside.

The house is at the lowest level of the gardens. Here also is the largest garden. This parterre garden—entered by means of a gate on the south side of the house—contains boxwood hedges that outline geometric flower beds. Each has a quince tree in the outer corner. In the center is the sundial. To the north of this level is a low stone wall with steps at either end leading to the middle terrace. Here is a promenade level bordered by crab-apple trees on one side and peonies on the other. (Spring is the recommended time for a visit.) There is also an herb garden on this level. The third level, edged by a retaining wall, includes hedges and ivies and other perennials. The entire garden is delightfully full—nowhere is there an impression of emptiness. In fact, the felicitous combinations of plantings and walkways, walls and steps, flowers and trees in such an intimate space makes this a fine example of what can be accomplished in the middle of a city—whether in the eighteenth or twenty-first century.

❀ **Admission:** Free.
Garden open: Both gardens are open daily year-round.
Further information: Hopkins House is located at the corner of Benefit and Hopkins Streets. Shakespeare's Head is at 21 Meeting Street.
Directions: The historic district of Providence is located just off I-95. Take the city hall exit in downtown Providence to South Main Street and the Brown University historic district. Benefit Street runs parallel to Main; Meeting Street crosses Benefit Street.

6. Ding Hao Garden

2105 Old Post Road, **South Kingstown,** RI

*I*N LATE SUMMER, visit Ding Hao, a very unusual garden off Route 110. Though it has all sorts of plantings on a couple of rocky, rustic hillsides, this place specializes in chrysanthemums. Dozens of varieties start blooming in August and continue through autumn—a sight to see (and to purchase if you wish). These hillside gardens are very diverse too, and are a good place to explore a very informal and delightful style of planting in a rocky, hilly New England landscape. Nothing is artificial looking. Plants and trees and rocks and garden shed and tools and you name it share this picturesque space.

❀ **Admission:** Free.
Garden open: Seasonally.
Directions: Ding Hao is at the corner of Ministerial Road (Route 110) and Old Post Road. It is in the part of South Kingstown called Perryville.

Don't Miss . . .

7. Rodman's Hollow

Cooneymus Road, **Block Island,** RI

IF MOORLAND and windswept island vegetation is your idea of natural beauty, this thirty-seven-acre wildlife refuge in one of New England's most unusual landscapes is well worth a visit. Here you'll find bayberries with their bright red berries and aromatic leaves, and wild roses in profusion. In particular note the rugosa rose, which blooms from June to September with a gloriously large rose-and-lavender blossom.

❁ **Admission:** Free.
Garden open: Seasonally.

8. Wilcox Park

Grove Avenue, **Westerly,** RI

THIS PUBLIC PARK is found behind the public library in the historic center of this oceanside town. A pleasant eighteen-acre expanse of flowers, shrubs, statues, fountains, and a duck pond, the quiet oasis was designed by Frederick Law Olmsted in the late nineteenth century. This is the perfect spot for a leisurely walk. You will find young mothers with small children in tow, workers on their lunch break, and other strollers enjoying the many shaded pathways.

After you walk, visit the Romanesque-style library—which has a public art gallery with changing exhibits—or take a stroll on Westerly's main street, lined with Gothic-style and Greek revival houses.

❁ **Admission:** Free.
Garden open: Year-round.

9. Smith's Castle

Route 1 (opposite state police barracks), **Wickford,** RI

www.smithscastle.org

THE SETTING of this historic house and garden is spectacular—a sweep of lawn right on a serene and unspoiled ocean inlet with rocks and waterfowl. The small 1678 colonial house—hardly a castle— where Roger Williams preached to the Indians is adjoined by a charming eighteenth-century garden. This prizewinning re-creation of a period garden was made using only plants from listings of the time, including globe amaranth, herbs, rose of Damascus, and gas plant dittany—all precisely set amid the boxwood borders of the colonial era. While in the neighborhood, be sure to visit the village of Wickford—a picturesque and historic spot.

❀ **Admission:** Fee.

Garden open: Daily except Thursday year-round; Sunday only in the afternoon.

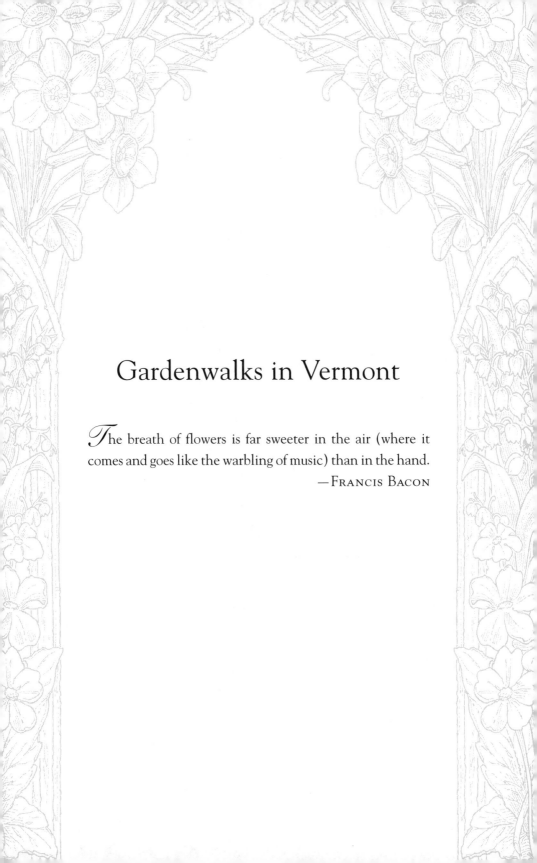

Gardenwalks in Vermont

*T*he breath of flowers is far sweeter in the air (where it comes and goes like the warbling of music) than in the hand.

—Francis Bacon

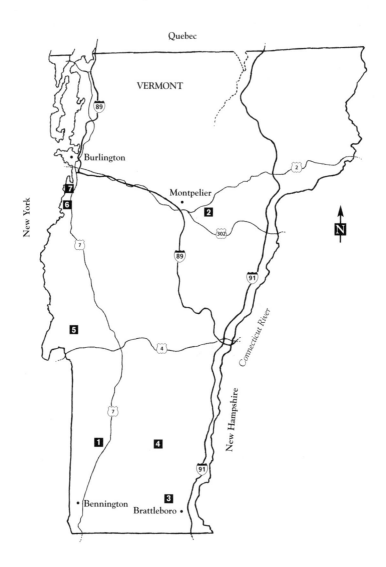

1. Manchester: Hildene
2. Plainfield: Great Woods
   Gardens at Goddard College
3. South Newfane: Olallie
   Daylily Gardens

Don't Miss . . .

4. Andover: Vermont
   Perennial Gardens

5. Bomoseen: Bomoseen
   State Park
6. Charlotte: Vermont
   Wildflower Farm
7. Shelburne: Shelburne
   Museum Garden

1. Hildene

Route 7A, **Manchester,** VT, (802) 362–1788, www.hildene.org

*P*ICTURE AN ELEGANT, formal plateau garden—brilliant with peonies—set dramatically between two Vermont mountain ranges with forested ravines and distant views all around. This unlikely—and very beautiful—setting is what you will find in a spring or summer visit to Hildene. Surrounding this formal garden are a variety of lovely landscape features laid out by the ubiquitous and always admirable firm of Olmsted and Company of New York: a great lawn, a hawthorne allée, walkways, woodland garden, and a pond. This is a great place at any time of year for a walk or even a cross-country ski outing.

The mansion with its spacious grounds in a pristine Vermont village was the summer home of Robert Todd Lincoln, son of the president. Various Lincoln descendants, including the president's grandaughter, Jessie, lived in the fine Georgian revival house until 1975. Having spent many years in England (her father was ambassador) and greatly admiring the gardens there, Jessie came back to Vermont around the turn of the twentieth century with an ambitious garden plan.

She laid out the formal garden design in 1907 on the plateau set so grandly between the Taconic and Green mountain ranges with the winding Battenkill river valley below. She apparently relished the contrast between the natural beauty of the surroundings and the formal organization of her garden. The great vistas in all directions—and all shades of green—accent the precision planting of the gardens in a most unusual way. We have rarely visited a garden placed so spectacularly within a naturally glorious setting.

Formal beds like these, however, take constant tending, and for more than forty years Jessie's garden was left in a chaotic, uncared-for state. By 1990 privet hedges had grown to 20 feet high, and the neat brick paths that intersect the gardens were covered inches deep with soil and grass. The hawthorne allée extending south from the house had filled in with vegetation. In the past few years, however, the gardens have been restored magnificently—some seventy-five-year-old peonies and fine old lilacs were even found still blooming—and today the garden you see is as close to perfection as constant gardening will make it.

This is a truly restored garden, for everything planted in it is a historically turn-of-the-twentieth-century kind of flower, and the original paths and flower-bed shapes are exactly as they once were. (Anyone interested in before-and-after garden restoration can inquire at the entrance desk; there are several articles describing in detail how such a historical reconstruction took place.)

The flower-bed design so lovingly re-created (and kept in order by dozens of volunteers) consists of a series of privet-edged squares and arcs, each with grassy centers and paths, resembling a maze. Each of the sixteen interconnecting beds was planted in a different color: four yellow, four pink, four white, and four blue. Each bed was surrounded with a (now severely trimmed) hedge. The overall effect was to resemble a vast stained-glass window; at the peak was the rose garden.

The plan has been ingeniously worked out: Each color is kept consistently abloom by a calendar of different flowers. The blue bed, for instance, contains lupine, delphinium, Siberian iris (spectacular), veronica, phlox, loosestrife, and blue-fringed daisies. (And that's just the list for June and July.)

We could tell you a great deal more about how this very precise garden idea is implemented. But perhaps it is best to advise visitors to see for themselves the lovely overall ambience of this most pleasing formality midst a glorious mountain setting.

Admission: Fee.
Garden open: There are daily tours of house and estate mid-May through October, and you can wander around the grounds from 9:30 A.M.
Directions: Manchester is located on scenic Route 7A. Either take Route 7A north from Bennington to about 7 miles beyond Arlington (entrance to Hildene on your right), or take Route 7 to the Manchester Center exit and take Routes 11 and 30, turning left (south) at the intersection with Route 7A. Go 2 miles to the Hildene entrance on your left, ½ mile past the Equinox Hotel.

2. Great Woods Gardens at Goddard College

Route 2, **Plainfield,** VT, (802) 454–8311
www.goddard.edu

TUCKED INTO the lovely Vermont greenery on a bucolic college campus is a very special garden. At the moment it is more architecture than plantings—or perhaps it is just more overgrown than most formal gardens. But that is part of its beauty. The structures of garden design are all very much intact, and as the current renovations continue, no doubt it will become quite a showplace. But as of our writing, this is much in the nature of a secret garden—a place with ineffable charm.

Great Wood Gardens were laid out in 1925 by the well-known and always artistic designer Arthur Shurcliff. Willard Martin was the owner of the estate that became Goddard College in 1938. His gardens were as much an architectural statement as flower beds, and fortunately the stonework has remained remarkably intact, even as the gardens were quite abandoned. Although a renovation (by a student) took place in 1973, and was aided briefly by the college, it is only recently that real, serious restoration has begun.

This is a garden on several levels, each outlined with spectacular stonework. Mixed Vermont granite and slate have been elegantly crafted to create walls, fountains, summerhouses, arches, pergolas—and all the architectural splendor that converts a garden from just being flower beds into a work of art. At the north end of the upper garden, there is a deep circular pool with a canal that runs from a fountain. There are balustrades and small delicacies of carving. Stone steps lead down to the next level, where, surprisingly, five ram's heads high on a stone wall spurt water from above into another pool. From here, more steps lead to a formal (once elegant) rose garden, in which a still perfectly serpentine pattern of boxwood separates the rose bushes. This walled garden is delightful, though unkempt, and its setting—on a perfect axis with the upper garden —is jewellike: It nestles into the landscape like an antique heirloom lying in a velvet box.

The pergolas and a small stone teahouse are also part of the three-tiered design. (Note the small carved stone animals on each corner of the slate roof.) Each level has other repeated motifs as well—arched doorways, for example. All of this structural material makes the plantings—there are already several very pretty restored flower beds—seem unusually lovely. Come visit in the springtime, or in rose season, and sit on the curved stone bench in the upper garden. Here you can look down on the lower levels and capture the special pleasures of this small but quite perfect garden.

❀ **Admission:** Free.

Garden open: Goddard College is open year-round to visitors.

Further information: The garden is near the tennis court—just beyond the parking lot.

Directions: Plainfield is northeast of Montpelier. Take Interstate 89 to Montpelier (exit 8). Then take Route 2 east about 8 miles toward Plainfield. The entrance to Goddard is on your left.

3. Olallie Daylily Gardens

Marlboro Branch Road, **South Newfane**, VT, (802) 348–6614
www.daylilygarden.com

*T*HIS IS A garden literally in a meadow—one of those lovely green Vermont meadows surrounded by mountains and brooks. The owners took their flat six-acre meadow and turned it into a patchwork quilt of flowering daylilies and Siberian irises and other brilliant perennials. They sell these flowers (by catalog and on the spot), but the atmosphere is not at all commercial. In fact, as you wander freely along the grassy paths in this field of flowers, you have a sense of stepping into and through a Van Gogh painting of a flower farm.

Owned by the Darrow family, Olallie means "place where berries are found" in a West Coast Indian language. The flower farm has horticultural history. Its founder, Dr. George Darrow—who began growing daylilies in Maryland—was a horticulturalist and plant geneticist for the USDA. He started breeding daylilies for his own interest with astonishing success: Some fifty-nine varieties of *Hemerocallis* are now registered with the Olallie prefix. About fifteen years ago, his son transplanted many of the daylilies to the family farm here in Vermont, and this thriving flower farm was opened to gardeners and other visitors.

You are probably familiar with the bright orange daylilies so common on New England's roadways. But here they say you'll find some eight hundred varieties! Daylilies come in a great array of species, colors, sizes, and blooming times. They range from large shrubs that fill the back of a flower bed to the most delicate miniatures. A visit will introduce you to many hybrids and species (some of which workers will dig up before your eyes and hand over to you, to your surprise and delight). You will discover that you can have a daylily garden that blooms continuously from June until the first frost—or even longer if you live in a warmer clime than frosty

Vermont. (As you might guess, plants that bloom so profusely in Vermont's harsh climate are very hardy—like Vermonters.)

Daylilies come in delicious colors, described for example as "clear melon," "spidery red wine purple with near black eye and chartreuse throat," or "peach opalescent sheen." This display is truly an artist's pleasure. In addition to the flower farm, there is a nice old-fashioned perennial garden and a rock garden. And if you visit in August, you can pick some of their luscious highbush blueberries. Needless to say, anyone with an interest in growing daylilies will be welcome and advised here, but you need not be a prospective *Hemerocallis* grower to enjoy this gardenwalk.

❀ **Admission:** Free.

Garden open: 9:00 A.M. to 5:00 P.M. May to September. Closed on Tuesday and occasional other days, so call to be sure.

Directions: Take Interstate 91 north to Vermont, take the Brattleboro exit, then follow signs to Route 30 north. Take the turnoff for West Dummerston about 7 miles north. South Newfane is the next town after West Dummerston; follow signs. At the crossroads in the center of South Newfane, take Marlboro Branch Road (you'll see a sign indicating the Marlboro direction), and you'll find Olallie on your left after about a mile.

Don't Miss . . .

4. Vermont Perennial Gardens

263 Dorman Road, **Andover,** VT, (802) 875–2604

THIS IS A PARTLY private, partly commercial garden, but wholly lovely, particularly its rock-gardened hillside deep in the Vermont woods. The color and stillness here are very special. Visit in summer.

❀ **Admission:** Free.

Garden open: Seasonally.

5. Bomoseen State Park

West Shore Road, **Bomoseen**, VT, (802) 265–4242

PICTURESQUE Lake Bomoseen is encircled by 10 miles of trails, including a nature trail noted for its wildflowers in spring and summer. This is a great trail for wild roses, hepatica, jack-in-the-pulpit, bloodroot, wild asters, and such woody plants as ferns and mosses. There are yellow water lilies in pond shallows.

❀ **Admission:** Fee in season.
Garden open: Year-round.

6. Vermont Wildflower Farm

Route 7, **Charlotte**, VT, (802) 425–3500
www.americanmeadows.com/about.cfm

THIS IS A woodsy six acres of fields and forest, where the largest wildflower seed center in the East displays all the many different wildflowers that grow in this northern clime. Careful labeling and pleasant paths are nice for the kids too.

❀ **Admission:** Free.
Garden open: Seasonally.

7. Shelburne Museum Garden

Route 7, **Shelburne,** VT, (802) 985–3346
www.shelburnemuseum.org

THE GARDENS here are only a small part of the very large complex of Americana on display. The vast property does include a large lilac collection of some ninety varieties, roses, a medicinal herb garden, and a pretty perennial garden called the Bostwick Garden. It is a circular, walled, flower garden found between the real lighthouse and one of the antique houses of the some forty sites here.

✿ **Admission:** Fee.
  Garden open: Year-round; call for hours, fees, and tour information.

Choosing an Outing

ASIAN GARDENS

Maine
Abby Aldrich Rockefeller Garden
Asticou Azalea Garden

Massachusetts
Naumkeag

New Hampshire
Fuller Gardens

GARDENS THAT CHILDREN WILL ESPECIALLY ENJOY

Connecticut
Gillette Castle State Park

Massachusetts
Berkshire Botanical Garden
Stanley Park

New Hampshire
Lost River Nature Garden

Rhode Island
Green Animals
Kinney Azalea Gardens

CONSERVATORIES AND BOTANIC GARDENS

Maine
Wild Gardens of Acadia

Massachusetts
Berkshire Botanical Garden
Garden in the Woods
Sedgwick Gardens at Long Hill
Smith College
Tower Hill Botanic Garden

ESTATE AND FORMAL GARDENS

Connecticut
Bellamy-Ferriday Garden

Maine
Hamilton House Garden
Woodlawn, the Colonel Black
    Mansion and Gardens

Massachusetts
Castle Hill
Naumkeag
Sedgwick Gardens at Long Hill

New Hampshire
Fuller Gardens

Rhode Island
Newport mansions

Vermont
Hildene

GARDENS LAID OUT OR INSPIRED BY FAMOUS LANDSCAPE DESIGNERS

Connecticut
Glebe House Museum (Gertrude
    Jekyll)
Harkness Memorial State Park
    (Beatrix Farrand)

Maine
Abby Aldrich Rockefeller Garden
    (Beatrix Farrand)
Garland Farm (Beatrix Farrand)

Massachusetts
Castle Hill (Frederick Law
    Olmsted)
Codman House (Ogden
    Codman Jr.)

Glen Magna (Frederick Law
 Olmsted)
Naumkeag (Fletcher Steele)
Smith College (Frederick Law
 Olmsted)

Rhode Island
Hammersmith Farm (Frederick
 Law Olmsted)
Wilcox Park (Frederick Law
 Olmsted)

GARDENS WITH
GARDEN ROOMS

Maine
Asticou Azalea Garden

Massachusetts
Sedgwick Gardens at Long Hill

HILLTOP GARDENS

Connecticut
Caprilands Herb Farm
Glebe House Museum
Harkness Memorial State Park
Laurel Ridge Foundation

Maine
Celia Thaxter's Garden
Thuya Lodge Garden

Massachusetts
Berkshire Botanical Garden
Glen Magna
Sedgwick Gardens at Long Hill
The Vale

New Hampshire
Aspet
Moffatt-Ladd House and Garden

Rhode Island
Hammersmith Farm

ITALIANATE GARDENS

Connecticut
Harkness Memorial State Park

Massachusetts
Codman House
Glen Magna
Sedgwick Gardens at Long Hill

GARDENS OF
NOTABLE AMERICANS

Connecticut
Gillette Castle State Park
 (William Hooker Gillette)
Nook Farm (Mark Twain and
 Harriet Beecher Stowe)

Massachusetts
Adams National Historic Site
 (John Adams)
Longfellow House (Henry
 Wadsworth Longfellow)

ORIGINAL AND
ECCENTRIC GARDENS

Connecticut
Caprilands Herb Farm
Gillette Castle State Park

Massachusetts
Castle Hill
Hammond Castle
Naumkeag

PRIVATE GARDENS

Connecticut
Garden of Susan and Robert
    Beeby

New Hampshire
Mr. Jacquith's Garden

ROCK GARDENS

Massachusetts
Stanley Park

New Hampshire
The Fells

ROMANTIC GARDENS

Connecticut
Gillette Castle State Park

Massachusetts
Glen Magna
Hammond Castle

New Hampshire
Barrett House

ROSE GARDENS

Connecticut
Bellamy-Ferriday Garden
Elizabeth Park

Massachusetts
Stanley Park

New Hampshire
Fuller Gardens

Rhode Island
Rosecliff (Newport Mansion)

GARDENS WITH SCULPTURE

Connecticut
Stamford Museum and
    Nature Center

Massachusetts
Butler Sculpture Park
Chesterwood

New Hampshire
Aspet

SPECIALTY AND THEMATIC GARDENS

Connecticut
Adam's Garden of Eden
Caprilands Herb Farm
Cricket Hill Garden (peonies)
Laurel Ridge Foundation
    (daffodils)

Maine
Asticou Azalea Garden

Massachusetts
Butterfly Place
Heritage Museums and Gardens
  (rhododendrons)
Newbury Perennial Gardens

New Hampshire
Rhododendron State Park

Rhode Island
Kinney Azalea Gardens

Vermont
Olallie Daylily Gardens
Hildene (peonies)

TOPIARY GARDENS

Rhode Island
Green Animals

VINEYARDS

Connecticut
Stonington Vineyard

WALLED OR INTIMATE GARDENS

Maine
Hamilton House Garden
Woodlawn, the Colonel Black
  Mansion and Gardens

Massachusetts
Codman House
Isabella Stewart Gardner Museum

New Hampshire
Fuller Gardens
Moffatt-Ladd House and Garden

Rhode Island
Shakespeare's Head

Vermont
Great Woods Gardens of
  Goddard College

GARDENS WITH WATER VIEWS

Connecticut
Cricket Hill Garden
Gillette Castle State Park
Harkness Memorial State Park
Laurel Ridge Foundation

Maine
Asticou Azalea Garden
Celia Thaxter's Garden
Hamilton House Garden
Thuya Lodge Garden

Massachusetts
Castle Hill
Hammond Castle
Ipswich River Sanctuary
Maudslay State Park
Parker River National
  Wildlife Refuge

Rhode Island
Blithewold Gardens and
  Arboretum
Hammersmith Farm
Newport mansions

WHEELCHAIR ACCESSIBLE GARDENS

Maine
Merryspring
Wild Gardens of Acadia

Massachusetts
Arnold Arboretum

Berkshire Botanical Garden
Chesterwood
Codman House
Heritage Museums and Gardens
Isabella Stewart Gardner Museum
Longfellow House
Naumkeag
Sedgwick Gardens at Long Hill
Smith College

New Hampshire
Aspet
Fuller Gardens
Strawbery Banke

Rhode Island
Green Animals
Newport mansions
Wilcox Park

WILDFLOWER AND WOODLAND GARDENS

Connecticut
Fairchild Connecticut Wildlife
    Gardens
Larsen Sanctuary of Connecticut
    Audubon Society

Topsmead State Forest

Maine
Hamilton House Garden
Merryspring
Robert P. Tristram Coffin
    Wildflower Reservation
Wild Gardens of Acadia

Massachusetts
Garden in the Woods
October Mountain State Forest
Parker River National Wildlife
    Refuge
Pleasant Valley Wildlife Sanctuary

New Hampshire
Ossipee Lake and Heath Pond Bog
Plainfield Wildflower Sanctuary

Rhode Island
Rodman's Hollow

Vermont
Bomoseen State Park
Vermont Wildflower Farm

Garden Shows and Festivals

Connecticut
Hartford: Annual Connecticut
Flower and Garden Show
(February); (860) 529–2123
Meriden: Annual Daffodil Festival
(April); (203) 630–4259

Maine
Portland Flower Show (March);
(207) 225–3998

Massachusetts
Boston: New England Spring
Flower Show (March); (617)
536–9280
Boylston: Seven States Daffodil
Show (May); (508) 869–6111
Nantucket: Daffodil Festival
(April); (508) 228–0644
Northampton: Smith College

Annual Spring Bulb Show
(March), Annual Chrysan-
themum Show (November);
(413) 584–2700
Stockbridge: Berkshire Botanical
Garden Summer Festival and
Flower Show (August); (413)
298–3926

New Hampshire
Keene: Flower Show (March);
(603) 352–2253

Rhode Island
Newport: Newport Flower Show
(July); (401) 847–1000
Providence: Annual Rhode Island
Spring Flower and Garden
Show (February); (800)
766–1670

Vermont

Burlington: Intervale Festival
(September); (802) 660–3505
Shelburne: Lilac Festival (May);
(802) 985–3346

Vergennes: Annual Flower Days
Festival (July and August);
(802) 475–2311

Glossary

allée: A stately tree-lined avenue.

arboretum: A place where an extensive variety of trees are cultivated for scientific, educational, or ornamental purposes.

belvedere: A structure such as a summerhouse situated to command a view.

bosquet: A small grove or thicket.

botanical garden: A place where a wide variety of plants are cultivated for scientific, educational, or ornamental purposes.

butterfly garden: A garden in which flowers are specially chosen to attract butterflies.

classical garden: A formal garden whose aesthetic attitudes and values are embodied in ancient Greek and Roman design.

colonial garden: A garden designed or reconstructed in the colonial American style, with separate sections for flowers, fruit trees, vegetables, herbs, and various outbuildings.

conservatory: A greenhouse in which plants are arranged for aesthetic display and in carefully controlled climatic conditions.

cottage garden: A small, unpretentious garden featuring flowers and vegetables in a casual arrangement.

cup garden: A garden in ancient Chinese tradition, in which an object is framed by its surroundings.

demonstration garden: A garden whose purpose is horticultural education.

English garden: A naturalistic garden style first developed in eighteenth-century England, as compared with the more formal French style.

espalier: A fruit tree or shrub trained to grow flat against a wall, often in a symmetrical pattern.

folly: A whimsical garden structure that is decorative rather than useful.

formal garden: A garden in which nature is trained to adhere to geometric or other formal decorative principles.

garden rooms: Individual, self-contained, and separately designed sections of a larger garden.

gazebo: A free-standing roofed structure, usually with open sides, that provides a shady resting place in a garden.

grotto: A small cave or cavern or an artificial structure made to resemble one.

ha-ha: A sunken hedge or moat that serves as a fence without impairing the view.

Italianate garden: A garden in the Italian style, often featuring classical elements, statuary, and fountains.

knot garden: Elaborate planting of greenery, usually thyme or box, following the patterns of knots.

maze: A garden labyrinth: an intricate, deliberately confusing, patterned network of hedges and pathways, designed to entertain.

naturalistic garden: A garden in which the design attempts to imitate nature in its free form rather than to impose form upon it.

orangerie: A sheltered place, such as a greenhouse, used particularly in a cold climate to grow oranges.

parterre: An ornamental flower garden whose beds and paths form a pattern.

pergola: An arbor or passageway with a roof or trellis on which climbing plants are trained to grow.

pleasure garden: A garden such as a flower garden or park, designed purely for enjoyment.

promenade: A place for strolling in a garden.

rock garden: A garden in which rocks and plants are arranged in a carefully designed, decorative scheme, often featuring alpine plants.

shade garden: A garden featuring plants that grow best in shaded areas.

topiary garden: A garden in which live trees and shrubs are clipped into fanciful shapes.

water garden: A garden in which

ponds, streams, and other water elements, as well as plants that grow at water sites, are an integral part of the overall design.

wildflower garden: Usually a preserve, in which flowering plants grow in a natural, uncultivated state.

winter garden: A conservatory or other indoor garden that can be enjoyed all year.

Zen garden: A garden in the Japanese tradition, designed for beauty and contemplation.

Index of Gardens, Landscapes, and Notable Designers

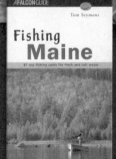
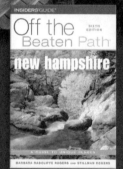